METAMEMOIRS
PERRY GLASSER

Outpost19 | San Francisco
outpost19.com

Copyright 2012 by Perry Glasser.
Published 2012 by Outpost19.

Glasser, Perry
  metamemoirs / Perry Glasser
  ISBN 9781937402457 (pbk)
  ISBN 9781937402464 (ebook)

Library of Congress Locator Number: 2012920055

OUTPOST
19

Also by Perry Glasser

SUSPICIOUS ORIGINS

SINGING ON THE TITANIC

DANGEROUS PLACES

RIVERTON NOIR

Acknowledgements

Gimme Shelter appeared in *Confrontation*
Helplessly Hoping appeared in *Memoir and...* as Excelsior
Hey Joe appeared in *The Portland Review*
Hungry Like the Wolf appeared in *The Antioch Review*
I'm Free appeared in *ACM*
If I Can't Have You appeared in *North American Review*
L.A. Woman appeared online in *Ekleksographia #3*
Layla appeared in *Boulevard* as "Yolanda"
Norwegian Wood appeared in *Confrontation*
parts of Jessica appeared as "Iowa Back Dirt"
in the *Good Men Project Anthology*
Silver Dagger appeared in *Northwest Review*
Stairway to Heaven appeared online in *Ekleksographia #3*
Sweet Dreams of You appeared in *Salamander* as "Video Girl"
The Times They Are A Changin' appeared in *Phi Delta Kappan*
as Not Half, Not Some
Thunder Road appeared in *GSU Review*
and
special appreciation to
the Virginia Center for the Creative Arts,
and The Norman Mailer House

Disclaimer

This book is based on memory, that inexact realm where impressions, surmise, and feelings replace history. I have written without malice. Where I have erred in fact, I apologize for any injury. The fault is wholly mine.

Perry Glasser

Perry Glasser is the author of four prior books of prize-winning prose. *Riverton Noir* was recipient of the Gival Press Novel Award (2012); *Dangerous Places*, a short fiction collection that received the 2008 G.S. Sharat Chandra Prize from BkMk Press (2009); *Singing on the Titanic* (Urbana and Chicago: The University of Illinois Press, 1987) a book recorded by the Library of Congress for the blind, and *Suspicious Origins*, short fiction, winner of the Minnesota Voices Competition (St. Paul: New Rivers Press, 1984). In 2012 he was named a Fellow of The Massachusetts Cultural Council for Creative Nonfiction/Memoir (2012).

He has been in residence at The Norman Mailer House, The Virginia Center for the Creative Arts, Yaddo, and Ucross, earned his MFA in Fiction at the University of Arizona, and teaches professional writing at Salem State University. He makes his home in Haverhill, Massachusetts.

You were loved with a full heart.

METAMEMOIRS

Origins

Norwegian Wood	1
Silver Dagger	13
Gimme Shelter	28
Hey Joe	52
Helplessly Hoping	74

Chalk

The Times They Are A-Changin'	94
Layla	102
If I Can't Have You	123
Stairway to Heaven	130
I'm Free	137

Still Looking

Love Has No Pride	154
Thunder Road	176
L.A. Woman	190
Sweet Dreams of You	196
Hungry Like the Wolf	203
Jessica	218
Somebody to Love	245

"…cut out the gentlemanly stuff
and tell us the story of your life."
—Nathanael West

"Of course, I do occasionally arouse primeval
instincts, but I mean, most men can do that."
—Mick Jagger

Origins

Norwegian Wood
The Beatles

Unless you grew up during the musical nuclear winter of "Help Me Rhonda," or "Sweet Little Sheila," or "Stay With Me, Diana," you cannot imagine the effect of first hearing "Norwegian Wood." Those earlier unrelenting '60s songs named for girls delivered me to uneasy longing. If Venus in blue jeans could redeem my worthless soul, why wasn't I in love?

Lennon's song about a random, meaningless, forgettable intersection of two lives was far closer to my life than any avowal of devotion made by Fabian, Dion, or Frankie Avalon. Lennon is unsure if he had a girl or if the girl had him; the girl takes him home, they drink some wine, and when he awakens alone *this bird had flown*. Before "Norwegian Wood," I was morally defective; Lennon's lyrics made it likely that dispelling ambiguity in pursuit of sense was a waste of time. *Meaning* was the arbitrary imposition of mind on discrete, random episodes. *Karma* vibrated into everyone's consciousness on the strings of George Harrison's sitar.

At the Club, the songs by pompadoured singers sucked dimes from our pockets into a Wurlitzer jukebox. It was the genuine article, plastic and glitz, filled with 45 rpm records. I was the jerk who sometimes pressed the buttons for "Norwegian Wood." Other guys held their noses and, though they knew, asked aloud, *Who played that shit?* At least it wasn't the Singing Nun. Any fool who pressed the buttons for the Singing Nun risked injury.

The Club was a poolroom above a pizza parlor and a dry cleaner on Kings Highway in Brooklyn. The place had a name—I can't remember it exactly, but it was something grand, stenciled on the windows over the street, maybe the Flatbush Chess, Checkers, and Billiard Emporium. The majesty of the name did not matter. What mattered was the fiction that the place was a club, a fine point that evaded some zoning ordinance. Poolrooms were well known dens of iniquity, but a club, well, that was the kind of place stalwart young gentlemen practiced gentility. In reality, no one held any illusions about the Club's exclusivity. Ambiguity was a virtue for art *and* commerce. The village idiot and Paddy's pet pig could buy membership if they put five dollars up front. Instead of the $1.25 per hour paid by guests, members paid $1.10. After 100 hours of shooting pool, you'd save $15.00. The more you played, the more you saved.

I saved a fortune.

I was 16, a senior at James Madison High School two years ahead of schedule. My parents had confused my education with a footrace, so I had started school young. When I later blew away a citywide test, my parents learned I was qualified to be allowed to skip 8th grade, a situation from which they drew considerable pride, but which also not-so-incidentally left me forever socially retarded, never quite one with my classmates.

Since I was bright, my high school teachers who designed student schedules had me assist them. It was a labor intensive job. There were no computers to screw up student and teacher programs. Screwing up student and teacher programs was accomplished manually. In my senior year, my teachers looked the other way when I scheduled myself into the expected top track academic classes, but somehow omitted such distractions as lunch, study hall and, by virtue of my being on the swimming team, gym class. The final effect of this mildly illegal scam was that after an hour of wind sprints and flip turns at dawn, I reported to my first class, AP Physics, at 8:00 a.m. and finished my last class, AP Calculus, at 11:30.

No juvenile delinquent, I did not wander the streets endangering society. The Club's doors were unlocked by Benny at noon. He'd greet me where I waited in the stair alcove, I'd follow him up, and while he opened the cash register I improved myself by studying Benny's copy of *The Daily Racing Form*. Benny was the Club's sole employee, a balding guy who chewed an unlit cigar, had eyebrows like leafless shrubs and a tuft of steely gray hair bristling from each nostril. He never emerged from behind his desk. He'd come to value my estimation of the ponies when I'd explained speed ratings to him, those fifths of a second off the track record at the distance expressed as two or three digit numbers, simple arithmetic to me, inscrutable to him. Later, when the usual crowd drifted in, I'd practice the mysteries of draw, follow, and how English could be employed to widen the angle of a bank shot.

You might assume the egghead brownnose kid would have the snot kicked out of him in that environment, but since I had earned the varsity letter sewn to my team jacket, and since I smoked Marlboro and chewed Sen-Sen to sweeten my breath, and since I once ran seventeen consecutive balls at straight pool while one of those cigarettes languidly hung from my lower lip, and since whenever I wrote sports for the school newspaper I transformed the Club's more athletic members to legends by dubbing them with nicknames like "Sweetshot" and "Ironman," my presence was grudgingly tolerated—provided I offended no one by reading Kafka in public.

The best player at the Club was a slight, tall boy named Arnie. Arnie's s long, fine fingers curled into a bridge so natural for a pool cue that the rumor his digits each had an extra joint seemed credible. Arnie was good enough to travel in search of opponents willing to play for money, and so Jackie, a furrow-browed defensive linesman for the school football team, shadowed Arnie. Arnie was no hustler—his reputation preceded him, making any deception to raise the stakes impossible. Having Jackie lurking nearby was simply prudent. If Arnie played in a strange neighborhood, he could carry a few hundred dollars in his pocket. Jackie was protective muscle.

Jackie let it be known as a matter of fact that if the two of them were hard up for cash, they might raise a stake by travelling to Greenwich Village where Arnie would beckon to some fag and lead him down an alley to where Jackie waited to relieve the poor bastard of his wallet. This was years before the Stonewall Riots in New York City changed the status of homosexuality from shame to lifestyle, and "gay" still meant "merry" that as an adjective might be applied to a woman's scarf. Arnie did not deny Jackie's story, and I believed it. I'd seen Jackie in a fit of rage at a missed shot throw a 4-ball across the room where it caught some guy in the sternum. The guy collapsed like a house of cards in an earthquake. Mind you, Jackie had no beef with the victim; the schmuck was just standing in the wrong place at the wrong time.

By May, we were so close to the end of high school, nothing mattered. The day was perfect. I sat on one of the high, red vinyl upholstered armchairs and leaned precariously back against a wall beside Benny's counter, a hint of daylight seeping past the opaque whitewashed windows. I'd walked through glorious spring light before climbing the dim stairs to the Club. I was young enough to assume that the number of such afternoons that would come to me was limitless, and so I could squander such a day without regret. Benny and I smoked my cigarettes when he laid his unlit cigar aside, and we made a meal of the potato chips I rattled and slapped out of a vending machine.

In front of us, Dennis banged the balls around a table as hard as he could. Not even point-and-shoot, just machine-gunning with a cue. "What in fuck are you doing?" I asked him, and without looking up Dennis said, "Practicing my luck." *Slam slam slam*. I glanced at Benny, who shrugged. As long as Dennis paid for his time and never rested a burning cigarette near the felt, Benny could not care less. You can practice bank shots; you can practice rail shots. Who is to say you cannot practice luck?

That day when Arnie and Jackie charged up the stairs, they hooted and hollered like the high-spirited adolescent boys they were. "Smell my lips!" Jackie shouted. "Smell my lips!" A small crowd of the regulars gathered around them to hear the story.

They'd cruised in Arnie's father's truck and managed to pick up two girls. "Italians," Arnie added, "the kind with the hair piled up on their heads." They did not know these girls. The girls were not from the neighborhood, but though I too did not know these girls named Donna and Anna-Louise, I knew just what they looked like. Too much make up, bangs over acne, rock-hard tiny asses, hip-hugging short skirts, black pantyhose, unsteady on 3-inch heels, tits like new apples, mascara that might have been applied with a trowel, and a simple gold cross on a fine chain resting over the pulse at the base of their slim throats.

I wanted and was terrified of these girls. Smelling of musk, their black-dyed hair rolled on beer cans and lacquered rigid, they beckoned in my restless dreams. No such girl had ever been seen in AP Physics. It is doubtful any ever enrolled in Calculus. To be sure, none ever sat in Problems of American Democracy. Arguably, they *were* problems in American democracy.

Arnie told us how they pulled up to a corner and asked these two girls if they wanted a ride. The girls laughed and got in the truck, and then they drove the truck someplace, and since these were good Catholic girls who planned to wear white when they married, they would not fuck, but they all agreed they could get naked. Which they did. "We oral sexed them and they blew us." For proof, Jackie dropped his pants to show us the cuts on his dick. One of the girls wore braces.

Dennis was amazed. Practicing luck suddenly seemed sensible. He asked again to hear the part when they switched girls and Jackie again shouted, "Smell my lips!" We were sure the story was true. Who would cut up his own dick just for a little juice with the guys?

No doubt, Arnie and Jackie, who entice and roll fags for money and so are about as close a life form to lichen that I know, have scored with two tarts. I will suffer many bad nights pondering their luck and the universe's injustice.

But I also know Arnie's father is a butcher. The back of his truck on a day as warm as this must reek of blood—beef, chicken, lamb, and pork. I imagine the tangle of naked limbs rolling around on the truck floor; I imagine sticky squares of brown butcher's paper.

Imagining details that make events more true, the sensory details others might omit or may simply never have noticed, is to become my life's habit. I have no idea why.

In that time and in that place, imagination is no gift. Mind you, I was unable to flip the pages of the *Sunday New York Times Magazine* without a brassiere ad engendering an erection. I never raised my hand in class for fear that if a teacher called on me and I had to walk to the chalkboard, my ever-present hard-on would be visible through my tight pants. I lived for warm school days in hopes that the lovely, smart, wholesome girls just a little older than I would wear sleeveless blouses so that as they moved and did wholesome, ordinary things, the material at their shoulders and arms would gap and offer to my hungry eyes a flash of paler, wholesome flesh.

Imagination has never made my life any easier.

After hearing Jackie and Arnie tell their story for a third time, adding important, fresh details with each telling, I swore I smelled the butcher's blood myself. I slid away from the crowd and headed down the stairs out of the Club into the stark afternoon light.

When I first thought to write this, when I came to this point in the process, for weeks I toyed with introducing Ellen, the girl with the Chiclets smile who captained my high school's cheerleading squad. I was mad for her. We were friends, but she was dating a guy in college, so my feelings for her were hopeless. I planned a sharply etched scene where Ellen and I spoke. I'd invent a pretext for us to meet. I'd twist a fact to put the Club in a basement, thereby making my departure an ascent into light from darkness, and on the street Ellen and I would talk about summer plans or college fears as we walked together, doing anything clean to stand in sharp relief to my grimy life left in the poolroom below. To make an unequivocal distinction between what was sordid and ugly and what was uplifting, I thought that in the moment I opted for the light, I'd have Ellen touch my cheek, a gesture roughly analogous to a touch she once truly gave my neck that I can still feel if I remember hard enough. Later still, I thought to write a final scene set on the tarpaper and gravel rooftop of the apartment building where I lived. There, on the day of graduation, overlooking all of Flatbush, the trees, the neat houses, the broad boulevards, I would dedicate my life to Art, snap my two-piece pool cue over my knee, and from the splinters, I would build a fire.

Stories want action precipitated by a character trait that generates a change of consciousness. In this case, the introduction of a woman as redemptive principle supports the change. The payoff roof scene would be set highest in the story's physical and thematic geography, from basement, to street, to rooftop, from base carnality, to romantic longing, to Art. While describing the fire, my broken pool cue, and my impulse for the pure and the beautiful, I'd deliberately omit writing, "Isn't it good, Norwegian wood."

If I'd done my work well, the line's absence would invite you, the reader, to supply it. By seducing and flattering you into participating in the creation of that resonance by adding an old sentence to a new context, you would invest the story with depth and meaning to elevate it above mere anecdote. You'd admire the piece because it conned you into thinking you were as clever and wise as the writer, your coconspirator in making sensible a senseless world. You'd recommend this writer, this artist, Glasser, to your friends, for his profound insight, his great heart, his compassion, so knowing, so candid, his wisdom so uncannily like your own. You and I…well, we'd be lovers of a sort.

But I don't write a lot of fiction anymore. Manipulating readers by organizing events into schema that make meaning isn't hard work, just dishonest.

I report.

None of that with Ellen actually happened, so I cannot write it.

You'll read about other women in these narratives. They are neither redemptive forces nor forces of any other kind. They are people. In this exploration of memory and heart, most of the women you will read about are younger than I am; several met in circumstances of which the Correctness Cops would disapprove. I am unapologetically heterosexual without being a predator. Love is where you find it, or in my life, where love finds me.

I try to be decent, but in a lifetime of shifting definitions, maintaining decency is daunting. In the arc of this book's memoirs and riffs, being decent in 1970 meant something very different from what it meant in 1990, and by 2010 it was wholly different again. It is assuredly indecent to insist that women are incapable of sexual self-determination and therefore require protections. As a father to a daughter, I insist on the distinction between *women* and *girls*. I also note that strength of will is not marked by a moment on a calendar.

The women who have opened my heart widest have been far stronger than I. One specifically and unequivocally pushed away from a table as she refused to be a symbol for me, ending any and all entanglements with me and my imagination. Cursing, my first wife made it plain she would not live in a Russian novel: my need to confess did not perforce her need to forgive. While a few women that I have loved may seem to redeem my worthless soul, I assure you, the assignment of that meaning is a trick of perception.

So I try to subscribe to a simple ethical standard. I recommend it to you.

Protect the weak; do not lie for advantage.

I've selected details, but not in service to some grander vision. I try to get the facts right, to tell the tale and do the story justice. These things happened. I bear witness. No nostalgia; no lessons learned; no inspiring triumph over adversity. Stories. Accuracy is a high standard, truth an accident, and wisdom an unapproachable ideal. Art? Well, I confess, I hope for that. Arranged right, words ought to make beauty.

You will find opinions unavoidably embedded within the tales themselves. I am not ignorant of how the selection of detail can shape sensibilities. I accept that responsibility and the consequent risk. You are alerted. For example, I agree the boys in the poolroom are repellant. Perhaps the girls need not have been identified as Italian, and perhaps I need not have mentioned the gold crosses at their throats. I regret any offense, but the affront, like meaning itself, lies in your mind, not on the page. It was 1965. They were boys. It was Brooklyn.

The soundtrack of my life suggests these narratives. Instead of a rounded story called "Graduation," you've read an inconclusive tale called "Norwegian Wood." Other riffs on other songs in other tempos will tell other tales. I am a product of my time; in my time, in America in the second half of the twentieth century, popular music defines us.

I write memoir, not history. Writers who attempt autobiography bewilder me, and I am in awe of the few who have believably managed it. So another witness may protest that what I report is only tenuously related to the facts. *Glasser, it happened* this *way, not* that.

In every case, they are right.

The truth I report and you read is the truth of the heart. If you find meaning in any of that, I am glad for you.

I still have my pool cue. As a matter of record, I will tell you that a few years after they nailed the tarts in the butcher's truck, when Jackie took a wrong step, a landmine vaporized the bottom half of his body. His blood drained into a rice paddy. He lived a few terrible seconds and then he was dead. Arnie, I believe, became a podiatrist. I haven't a clue as to where or what Ellen does.

Meaning. Isn't it good?

Silver Dagger
Joan Baez

My mother's breath fills my ear as she whispers from her deathbed, "That goddam bitch Joan Baez ruined your life."

Muriel has told me this many times. She isn't senile; this is a theme of hers. I jet back to Massachusetts, and though she lingers longer than anyone predicts, in Florida a few weeks later, she dies in her sleep. The prior evening, when her nurse asked if she wanted anything in the morning, my mother joked, "I'll have a dry Martini."

So my brother and sister and I bury our mother with a fifth of Boodles Gin, a pint of Martini and Rossi Dry Vermouth, and a jar of green olives. Had we buried her with pearl onions, she'd have risen from the dead. "Who ordered a goddam Gibson?" she'd say. When I share my resurrection scheme with my sister, she thinks I am joking, but Muriel lived a life nourished by spleen; who knows how long enmity can animate the soul?

Joan Baez begins twisting my life in Abby's basement. Abby is at the center of a high school clique; I am at its periphery. If she is the Sun, I am Pluto or maybe Neptune. This is 1964. Five of us sit cross-legged around a single ashtray on a worn sand-colored carpet, marveling at *Silver Dagger*, a woman's lament at the perfidy of men.

> *My Daddy is a handsome devil.*
> *He's got a chain five miles long,*
> *On every link a heart does dangle*
> *Of another maid he's loved and wronged.*

Baez's voice is lovely, a pure call from a realm free of market surveys and hucksters. Our group experienced puberty when popular culture was about nothing. Not that it lacked meaning—it was deliberately and purposefully about nothing. Overdosing on *Ozzie and Harriet* and *Father Knows Best* induced a morphine-like stupor from which we awakened only during the turmoil of what people call The Sixties. That day in that basement, we are post-Elvis, pre-Beatles. The Rolling Stones are a mother's nightmare not yet dreamed. At parties in basements like Abby's we gyrate to gimmick dance tunes. *Mashed Potato Time, The Pony, The Bristol Stomp, The Twist*—all exercises that leave us flushed, exhausted, and safely virginal. None of these songs requires the dancers to touch. Romance and slow dancing are accompanied by fully orchestrated nasally sung numbers about vague longing for which no action is permitted, possible, or even imaginable. A whole subgenre of popular music is devoted to automobiles, engendering healthy, peppy enthusiasm for cars and drag racing. You can't do much with a good girl, but you can always twiddle a carburetor.

But here's this Joan Baez, severe straight black hair,

eyes sad and knowing, with the voice of a disappointed angel. She's nothing at all like Annette or any other Mouseketeer. *Silver Dagger* is the first song on the first side of her first album, and in it a girl denies a proposal of marriage and vows to sleep alone for all her life; her mother lies beside her armed with a silver dagger to defend her child from men, a precaution the mother takes because the girl's faithless father has fucked so many women.

To appreciate fully the impact of the moment in Abby's finished basement, compare that idea to one of our junior high school favorites, truly words to live by:

What is love?
Five feet of heaven in a ponytail.
The cutest ponytail
That sways with a wiggle when she walks,
(Sways with a wiggle, yes, a wiggle when she walks,
Sways with a wiggle when she walks.)

Baez unflinchingly hits the solid center of things where truth resides, and on the floor at Abby's, if none of us can articulate it, we already know it. Truth is potent stuff. Disdaining any orchestration, Baez strums guitar chords and sings about passion, betrayal, and death, the stuff of legend, the stuff that tells us what our lives will truly be.

No one speaks. When someone says, "Play it again," no one objects. Abby lifts the needle and places it at the song's beginning two, three, four times. Never mind the rest of the album; this song needs to be absorbed before we can move on. This is not background music. We are not here to dance. In fact, none of us will dance to music again for a decade.

My mother knew that this was a plot hatched in the Kremlin, a scheme to subvert youth away from Americanism by presenting us with unprocessed reality. Unaware of the intricacies of Khrushchev's nefarious purposes, we confidently smoke cigarettes, assured by doctors, baseball stars, cowboys and other authentic Americans on television that nothing could be more wholesome than smoking cured-in-Virginia tobacco. Menthol, we are informed, soothes the throat. We nonchalantly tap ash as if we have done so for years. I experiment with a European hold, my Marlboro between my thumb and forefinger, a bid for intensity I have formulated after seeing a photograph of Camus.

I am a high school junior. It is spring; next September and October when I am a senior, undeterred by rain, wind or hail, I will at rush-hour stand at the base of the stairs to a Brooklyn elevated train station to distribute flyers for the peace candidate, Lyndon Baines Johnson. Johnson promises he will never send an American boy to die in the place of an Asian boy. I am not old enough to vote, but as the party regulars at the neighborhood Democratic office load a canvas postal bag with forty pounds of literature for me to distribute, they say that activist 15-year-olds like me will save America from war.

The group Baez corrupts in Abby's basement is mostly composed of the children of Jewish lefties, the kind of people who send money to the NAACP, won't cross picket lines, and read magazines like *The New Republic* and the *Saturday Review*. My friends grow up familiar with Woody Guthrie lyrics sung by The Weavers; their parents schlep them to Lincoln Center to attend Leonard Bernstein's Youth Concerts.

My experience, however, was different.

My father prefers simple storytelling unmuddled by ideas. A painting contractor, he works hard with his back and hands. At day's end, the last thing he wants is befuddling text. So we subscribe to the photojournalism of *Life* and *Look*. Pictures never lie, right? Dad's favorite LP is a recording of Spanish bullfighting music; he likes the crashing cymbals. We also own a recording of Jackie Gleason conducting music for lovers. My parents' sole political conviction is that since authority figures have access to information we do not, and since they have our best interests at heart, as did Franklin Delano Roosevelt, our leaders require our unequivocal, unquestioning support. This happy perspective saves them from thinking about much of anything. So Lyndon Johnson is their kind of guy, though my mother snorts contempt when she tells me I am a *schmuck* for wasting my time handing out Johnson's literature without being paid. You can bet Lyndon is no fan of Joan Baez.

My experience also differs in that I do not live in the same neighborhood as my friends. Put two New Yorkers in a room, and they will fix each other's status and education by asking what high school they attended. In a city with 100 high schools, school zones serve the same purpose as town names in Kansas or Iowa or

Ohio. My friends live in homes; my family occupies an apartment. My friends have driveways that terminate in a backyard where likely as not a basketball hoop is affixed to the garage roof; my bedroom window looks across an alley to the blank brick wall of an adjacent building. My friends at night hear crickets; when I sleep with the window open, I can hear the squealing brakes of the elevated train five blocks away.

In 1964, I attend James Madison High because, at my mother's insistence, to get me admitted to that better school, my father contacted another family named Glasser with the "right" address. The telephone book reveals all he needs to begin the plot. A few dollars change hands; *voila!* the Board of Education is deceived. I travel by bike when weather permits, public bus otherwise. Meanwhile, the school mails letters about my absences, PTA meetings and all the rest to a David Glasser who is not my father.

One afternoon close to graduation, Abby is sent home from high school; she neglects to wear shoes. Subways, buses, sidewalks—all sorts of city grime blacken Abby's stubby toes. When her father is summoned to school, the guy protests his daughter's ejection. Abby's father teaches history at a community college, and so he qualifies as an intellectual. The news of a parent who tells our principal to go jump in a lake and that his daughter cannot be denied her education for violating a dress code is electrifying. No one believes it at first telling. He said *what?*

The world turns upside down. Had I told them of Abby's father's insubordination, my mother would have called the history professor a jerk, and my father would have called him a communist. Jerks and communists argue with school principals. But we live so far away, the gossip can never find my mother's ear at the beauty parlor or market. Besides, including her subway commute, she works a ten-hour day in an office in Manhattan, and so is far from the social circles of my friends' stay-at-home mothers. My older sister and brother are already married and gone, leaving me the only member of our five-person family ever to sleep in a room alone, a latchkey child before there was such a term.

At a time when girls' pastel-colored pants have zippers in back or at the side, Abby habitually wears faded men's dungarees. Snouts in the wind twitching at the scent of money to be made, the garment industry mints the word "jeans" for a generation swayed to the dark side by the likes of Joan Baez. "Dungarees" are for shoveling shit; jeans at least you can wear outside a barn. Abby buys her pants in the Boy's Department after scanning conversion charts to figure out which size will come closest to fitting the wider hips of a girl; she then wears her new pants in a cold bath, forcing them to shrink to her contours. No one manufactures women's jeans. What for? Surely, this fad will go the way of the flapper.

Though she has a lovely smile, Abby looks sourly unhappy most of the time. She graduates with perfect College Board scores, attends Barnard, and is unapologetic about being brilliant at a time when smart girls are reflexively deferential. If the boys around her felt stupid, Abby just did not give a shit. She and other nascent feminists were plainly victims of the wily Joan Baez, that pinko stooge loose in the land intent on destroying the moral fiber of America's women by inducing them to eschew pastels, turn to denim, put their zippers up front, and find fulfillment through accomplishment. Every patriot knows the plan for commie world domination needs the dominoes to fall. Get women strumming folk music and pretty soon they are leading their middle school kids in a march down Main Street singing The Internationale on May Day.

Shortly after I first hear Baez, my older brother finishes medical school, fulfilling our parents' ambitions for him. Baez perverts me from a similar straight and true path by singing mind-addling songs such as *Michael Row the Boat Ashore* and *The Battle Hymn of the Republic*. Such tunes drive medicine, dentistry, law or accounting right out of a young boy's mind. If that were not enough to draw up the indictment, Baez warbles through *We Shall Overcome*. My moral compass is destroyed; my soul is no longer my own.

No sooner does my brother finish his medical residency than he becomes a guest of the US Army. Trained as an obstetrician, he'd been assured he will spend his military service ministering to the needs of Army wives and female military personnel, perhaps in Stuttgart or some other cushy NATO outpost where better cognacs are served in the Base Exchange. But after a year at Fort McClellan, Alabama, he hauls his duffel bag and ass to Vietnam to join other American boys safe and free of the corrupting clutches of Joan Baez.

In the jungles of the Mekong Delta and the DMZ, they win hearts and minds by smoking tar heroin, fragging second lieutenants, and pacifying villages by burning thatch-roof huts to the ground.

My brother comes home whole in late 1966, but he is a profoundly changed man. Two years later, my draft lottery number comes up as Two-Digit Doom, a God-forsaken 50 for the love of Christ. *Why not fucking* one? I think. The draft lottery is marketed to the American public as an efficient and fair means for young men to know where they stand so they can get on with their lives instead of living with uncertainty. Get on with their lives? With my fucking 50 I have no life to get on with; my sorry ass is guaranteed to General Westmoreland's meat grinder unless the war ends before I graduate and lose my student deferment. "They have no air force and we are bombing them silly," my father reassures me. "Those napalm bombs … ." He shakes his head. He has seen big rosy blooms of flame immolating the jungle to black ash in the centerfold of *Life*.

Joan Baez subverts the war effort by refusing to pay the portion of her taxes that represents the military budget. This is her imitation of another Pied Piper of American youth, the mind-controlling stooge, fellow traveler and commie lackey, Henry David Thoreau. My well-off friends from better neighborhoods where magazines have words in them hire lawyers who employ every legal means to delay induction. I have friends whose parents pay expensive shrinks to discover insurmountable emotional problems in their sons. I have friends who every semester enroll in college classes and then before final exams deliberately drop all but six credits, an expensive tactic that allows them to maintain their student status and thus avoid being blown to small gobbets of flesh by a Claymore buried on a jungle trail. These are delaying tactics, but I even have friends whose parents personally drive them to Niagara Falls, walk with them across a bridge, kiss them, hold them fervently and say goodbye before sending financial support to banks in Montreal and Toronto. It's a bold, sad, and seemingly permanent act; these people cannot know that Jimmy Carter will years later order amnesty for sons who fled to Canada.

But I am set the task of beating the draft with no parental aid. It's not as though my parents are beyond duplicity—I attended the "wrong" high school for three years through their machinations. Still, I am on my own. Everyone I know has heard that if you swallow Juicy Fruit, the gum shows up as ulcers on an X-ray, but we also know that this tactic only buys thirty days and a second, more rigorous physical to be administered after 48 hours of isolation. Claiming homosexuality to beat the draft requires a positive answer to the question, "Have you experienced anal intercourse?" a tough one to lie about when you are 19, but even if you did manage to say "Yes," they bend you over and ask you to spread. A simple blowjob between friends just won't do. Death by landmine seems preferable to any plan that might fake the necessary physical evidence. And, as a Jew, I can forget claiming Conscientious Objector status. Just forget it.

Being a Yid and believably claiming a heritage of

pacifism is about as likely as having the Pope summon me to the Vatican to discuss the finer details of Jesus' *bar mitzvah*. Judaism and pacifism simply have no connection. Those Old Testament types were at war *all the fucking time*. If he'd had the option, that sapper David would have traded his leather sling for a Kalashnikov with a double banana clip before confronting Goliath. It is not impossible that the future poet-king of Judea took Goliath's ears and laced them on a leather cord he wore around his neck. No, being a Jew just puts C-O status beyond reach. Even if I could persuade a sympathetic draft board that my personal, nonsectarian brand of pacifism makes Gandhi look like Attila the Hun, all I'd earn for my trouble is a direct flight to the Big Muddy as a noncombatant. Being a noncom is no bargain: a medic under fire, crawling through mud, intent on saving the ass of some other dumb schmuck who could not figure out a way to beat the draft, has a very short life expectancy. To make sure the Jewish medic pussy attracts fire away from real soldiers, the Army will paint a Red Cross on my helmet, a bull's eye for some Viet Cong in black pajamas with a night scope. Without my own rifle, unless I am lucky enough to die of friendly fire, if I manage to survive some shitstorm I am guaranteed to wind up in a Viet Cong tiger cage, an insidious 2x2x2 bamboo box reserved for American POWs. My only comfort will be to know that while I ingest the protein available from the maggots picked out of my ulcerating sores and lose my teeth to scurvy, a cheerleader in Toledo or Minneapolis who wears my name etched on a steel bracelet might be going down on the captain of the football team. This seems very little compensation. Fuck C-O status. If this Jew-boy goes, he is taking a gun.

Recently my brother told me how he sent letters to our mother about the glorious life he led in country, a captain dining on steak and lobster in an air-conditioned hospital tent near the pink sand beach of Cam Rahm Bay; he also sent our father desperate pleas for rescue. The Army had reneged on its promises. In reality, my brother was in any number of firefights on a helicopter gunship. Call a congressman. Get a senator. But our father lifted no phones. He sent no letters. Dad, by the way, missed World War II by virtue of having two children, the same number my brother had when the Army shipped his ass out. As I write this, my brother is 64 years old. His eyes water when he tells me the tale. His lips pale. Our father never answered his letters, and when I tell my brother how Dad boasted to his neighbors about how his son the doctor was a Captain leading the life of Reilly, my brother mutters a curse and pours us both two more fingers of fine scotch.

But back in 1964 in Abby's basement, as I listen to that corrupting bitch, Baez, the peacenik my mother knows with utter certainty will ruin my life, it seems impossible that the war can last. More likely, my friends and I will live forever, join the Peace Corps, cure cancer, and reduce the workweek to 25 hours.

The summer of 1967, I handicap horses at Aqueduct, never get a haircut, lose my virginity, and work for my father. When he has work, Dad paints expensive places in Westchester and on Park Avenue. He's a fine craftsman, a favorite with a few upper-crust decorators, so the wealthy are his clientele. I paint the closets and fences in their expensive places. Dad pays me union scale, and though he grimaces when he sees me smoke a cigarette during lunch, he assures me he will not tell a workingman how to live. It's a matter of respect.

One August day as heavy rain snakes greasy tracks on the windshield of his small truck, we drive home on the twisting, elevated West Side Highway. The radio news routinely reports the daily body count. "Didn't your father leave Austria to avoid being in the army of the Emperor, Franz Josef?" I ask, a topic that used to engender a guffaw and a yarn, but this day Dad stares into traffic. It's the rain, I figure. He needs to concentrate.

"Your father avoided the draft, right, Dad?" I repeat.

"Your brother went," he says without turning his head to see me. "You'll do your duty." I am 19. The hard rain falls on the truck roof. The West Side Highway ramp down to the Brooklyn Battery Tunnel was paved with cobblestones, treacherous in wet weather, a bitch at rush hour. Dad's eyes stay locked on the road.

In 1968, when I am 20, people like my parents fight to be first in line to vote for Tricky Dick Nixon because he has a secret plan to end the war. Every state in the Union, save Massachusetts, goes for Dick. Look, the Democrats had got us into this mess, Lyndon Johnson was a lying fuck, Robert Kennedy was iced in June, Eugene McCarthy was a freaking poet, and party-stalwart

Hubert Humphrey had been going down on Lyndon. Besides, who could vote for anyone named *Hubert*? But Nixon has a secret. Nixon knows more than we do, right? His plan is so fucking secret, not even Nixon knows what in holy fuck it is. A picture of Nixon's plan in *Life* or *Look* would be an immaculately white, shiny blank page. *Perfect!*

A mere six years later, a full decade after I first hear Joan Baez in Abby's basement, America watches Nixon's secret plan play out. They voted for it, and there it is! As Communists overrun Saigon, the last American helicopter soars off the roof of the US embassy while desperate allies dangle from the helicopter's struts, US Marines club their grips loose with rifle butts, and our allies fall back to earth to certain imprisonment and probable death.

Is that a great plan, or what?

So back in the same season America first turns to Tricky Dick, nine months before I am to graduate from college, I opt for my only legal way to avoid being drafted. I enroll in three of the classes I need to obtain a teacher's license in New York City, a job that offers something called an Occupational Deferment. New York City public schools hunger for male teachers. I figure I can hide out in classrooms for a year or two. I will delay. Once the war ends, I plan to follow my heart's desire; hitchhike around America to learn what Kerouac knew, maybe write a book.

Delay of my heart's desire becomes a theme of my life.

Abby went to law school. So did her boyfriend,

Joshua, whose pinhole hernia made him 4-F, unfit for induction, but left him nevertheless capable of delivering a wicked overhead smash when he played tennis for Columbia University. Marty had psoriasis. Larry had flat feet. Me? I am fucked by perfect health.

Two weeks before I walk into my first classroom in 1969, the Handmaiden of Ruin, Joan Baez, shows up at the Woodstock Festival of Music and Art. She bores 350,000 people mired in mud with a song about a union organizer, Joe Hill. But her dull set occurs right after Country Joe McDonald electrifies the same crowd in Yasgur's field by leading them in the Fish Cheer: *F-U-C-K!* Then Country Joe sang *I-Feel-Like-I'm-Fixing-to-Die Rag.*

> *Well, come on mothers throughout the land,*
> *Pack your boys off to Vietnam.*
> *Come on fathers don't hesitate,*
> *Send your boys off before it's too late.*
> *Be the first one on your block*
> *To have your boy come home in a box.*

Forty some-odd years later, I still stand before classrooms. My cheap watches regularly jam with chalk dust. My students wear jeans all the time, and they write pious essays about how anyone in America can become anything they want if they work hard enough. My students believe destiny is a matter of choice and effort. They know they control their lives.

Who would dare suggest otherwise?

Gimme Shelter
The Rolling Stones

"What is it about *goyim* and Jews?" Helena says to me. Her husband is making her *meshuggah* again.

"They're different," I say.

I imagine my ex-wife at the other end of the telephone line, 2,500 miles and thirty years away, nodding her head and chewing a few strands of her hair as she did when solving the Sunday New York Times Crossword Puzzle. Helena's hair still hangs to the small of her back, though it is peppered with gray and not as lustrous as it once was. We're divorced long ago, but you can't make new old friends, and so the two of us occasionally feel the need to schmooze.

Helena and I were raised in adjacent Brooklyn neighborhoods—Flatbush and Bensonhurst—but at the most precarious point in our marriage we grasped at the illusion that geographic relocation could remedy any amount of rot within the soul. We'd forgotten we were Jews. Jews don't get born again; what they do is cross an international border and hope to be allowed to be Jews. We'd had a child, two cars, a motorcycle, a mortgage, and a loveless marriage, but as Americans we assumed we could make our break and rekindle a new beginning. We equated mobility with change, and so we had gone west.

The daughter of two Jews who respectively fled Poland and Austria, Helena now lives quite a distance from the *shtetl*. A probation officer for Pima County, Arizona, from time to time she carries a .44 Ruger, the caliber of choice for Dirty Harry and the Son of Sam. Helena is married to a man ten years her junior from Council Bluffs, Iowa, a guy with jailhouse tattoos on his arms and chest, the kind done with a Bic pen and a straight pin on those long afternoons in the county lockup. Helena has two master's degrees and still can read a Russian novel for pleasure. The mother of three, she's a not-terribly-happy over-educated bureaucrat in failing health who spends her days among rapists, drug addicts, methadrine cooks, biker smuggling gangbangers and *feebs*—agents from the FBI or ATF. What's a nice Jewish girl doing in a place like that?

"But *why* are *goyim* different?" Helena asks, and in a voice that could have been her mother's adds, "This is what I want to know."

I like to sound certain, but in truth I have no idea what I mean when without missing a beat I say, "History."

Later, the one word seems terribly accurate but terribly perplexing. Helena's and my origins are very different, but from a dark place deep within who we are there's an unmistakable essence, a genetic identity that cannot coexist with an idea we both once unquestioningly accepted—the very American notion that people are free to reinvent who they are.

Such illusions are not for Jews. As I grow older, the only thing of which I am absolutely certain is that no one's life starts with birth.

Max and Minnie

Max and Minnie married shortly after they met in New York City in the 1940s. It was late in their lives.

Helena's parents were the first people I knew well that seemed to be real Jews. There's no other way to say it. Max walked to *shul* on Saturdays; Minnie lighted *shabbos* candles; Allen, their son, attended a *yeshiva* and so wore a *yarmulke* all the time. In contrast, my parents drove to the Reformed Jewish temple they attended only on the High Holy Days; on weekends, we went to Sheepshead Bay where my mother could order a very unkosher lobster. Though I was a bored discipline problem in elementary school and my parents were urged to send me to a private school better equipped to work with gifted children, the only one they considered was run by the Society of Friends. The fees were so astronomical, the public schools would simply have to do. No thought was given to a *yeshiva*.

Max's life had been hard and he never spoke about it, except to me, his son-in-law. I told him that as a writer I was always in search of material. Max believed that assisting his son-in-law in achieving his heart's desire was worth a bit of personal anguish. I was maybe 23 and now I shake my head, amazed at my pretension. Today, I'd ask for a kidney before I'd ask a man for the worst details of his life.

Max was generous to his daughter, Helena, and to me. Our wedding was to be a business event with more than 200 guests; Max had connections that needed to be invited. Helena and I, steadfastly '60s American urban hippies with visions of getting married barefoot on a beach or in a park at dawn, simply refused to have anything to do with planning the event. This did not prevent Max and Minnie from trying to involve us. Max asked what kind of music we wanted, the choice being between hiring a band that played *schmaltz* or one that played what was called "society." I facetiously said, "The Rolling Stones." At the time, His Satanic Majesty, Mick Jagger, had positioned the Stones to be the Dionysian counterpoint to the very Apollan Beatles. Rumpled and always two rungs beneath decency, the Stones were misogynist, appealing counterpoints to the adorable mop-tops. Who could feel threatened by Ringo? High school girls squealed and giggled over which of the Fab Four was cutest, but the only question surrounding the Rolling Stones was which band member was the most depraved. For every "Michele" or "Yesterday," Keith and Mick crafted a "Stray Cat Blues" or "Under My Thumb." But by 1970, when Helena and I married, my personal favorites were their quasi-political riffs, "Sympathy for the Devil," "Street Fighting Man," and the very amazing "Gimme Shelter." The songs resonated with my personal anger, an amalgam of political disgust and my more personal distrust of all authority. I was trapped in a culture of fools that was trying to kill me, and I took that very, very personally. I was sure I knew the face of evil.

Max and Minnie, what could they know about evil?

Max being Max, when I suggested the Stones as a wedding band, he reached for his wallet. "How much could these Rolling Stones want?" he asked. Anything to keep the peace. His son, Allen, had to explain that I'd been sarcastic.

For his wife, Minnie, and his son, Allen, Max's generosity was more rare. In the end, that difference in treatment made for a lot of *tsouris* between Helena and her brother, the origins of a family drama as familiar as King Lear and at least twice as old. Money may not be the same as love, but in some families, it is the currency of the heart.

Naturally, since Max confided his history in me, Helena wanted to know the secrets of Max's pre-American life as he revealed them. Allen seemed not to give a shit, but that may be because at the time he was just a kid, a *yeshiva bucha* who rolled his eyes and giggled like a girl if he had to take his parents seriously; he much preferred to consider them as vaguely comic figures who, like Bela Lugosi, could not pronounce the letter "w."

Minnie was ambivalent about Max's past, at once curious and terrified of the details. She'd borne the man two children and never really knew him. I'd shared a hotel room with Max just once, and so I knew what Minnie knew, which was that in his sleep Max shouted and wept in Polish, his arms wildly waving above him as he fought God-knows-what demons. Minnie, Austrian, spoke little Polish. Her voice was thick with Viennese German. She and her husband communicated in English or Yiddish, and neither was a master of either.

In their close kitchen, Minnie and I often sat at the

Formica table where Minnie played a perpetual game of solitaire. Something with the aroma of boiled socks was always on the stove. The kitchen had the fetid feel of an unattended steam room gone cold. The tiny table was piled with shirts that needed collar buttons, unopened mail, and a sticky, tattered deck of blue diamond-back Bicycle playing cards with a dog-eared ace of spades. I never saw the ashtray clean. A cigarette hanging from her lip, without looking up at me, she'd say, "*So, nu?*" a query that made it clear she was willing to hear from me a bit of what I was collecting on audio tape. Minnie would sweep her graying hair from her eyes and brush the ashes that fell from her Kent to her chest. "So? Max. What did he say?" she'd add, but still not dare to look up.

"I'll let you know when we finish talking," I'd say. That answer kept her happy and me off the hook.

We smoked and drank coffee together from the moment I started seriously dating Helena. Later, as Minnie's son-in-law who shared cigarettes, drank black coffee and had shown her two variations of Solitaire she did not know, I was good company, likely the only man in her life that ever paid her any attention beyond a glowering expectation of food or laundry service.

Minnie had escaped Europe on the *Rotterdam*, the last ship to sail from Austria before the *aunchlauss*, not because she feared Hitler's Final Solution ("We heard things, but they sounded so crazy who could believe them?"), but because she'd belonged to the Young Socialist League. That red stain on her record would make it impossible for her to find work under National Socialism. Her immediate family with less radical politics stayed confidently behind. They met extermination in Dachau.

Minnie would talk about her vanished world as if it were a place to which she might return. She'd been a schoolgirl who attended opera. She had had a lover who played violin. "It was Vienna," she explained to me and pushed her cigarettes closer, offering. Her father knew Freud. They went to shows, which she called "theyater." A handful of Minnie's cousins also survived. Members of a hiking club, days after Hitler annexed Austria, one afternoon, dressed in little more than lederhosen, they went hiking in the mountains. Months later, they stopped at the gates of Jerusalem. Helena had family in Israel.

Who could be more Jewish?

Max departed Old Europe less decidedly than Minnie. Max had a twin brother, Samuel, dead of starvation in the early 1930s. Her love of Russian literature's melodrama a point too strong, Helena envisions the uncle she never knew dying in her father's arms, but Max denied this tale to me, his son-in-law, the family chronicler. Max supplied no alternative details, however, insisting he could not remember. The memory lapse around his brother's horrible death was no doubt a choice, but even a pretentious 23-year-old filled with *chutzpah* acknowledged that certain details would have to be buried with Max.

Max made his first fortune in Brussels, a fact his wife and children knew and took for granted but which I found amazing. In my parents' house, making money was an Horatio-Alger-Yankee-Doodle dream that called for luck and pluck. You had to be in the right place at the right time, and who you knew was more important than what. Max however, went wherever he could survive, and when he got there he knew no one. Lots of pluck; no luck at all.

Max spoke fluent French. The geography of his tales troubled me enough that I asked Max how he made his way from Poland to Belgium. "I worked with a hook," was the best his English would do, pronouncing the verb *voirked*, and by gesture and my best guess established that he toted cargo on the ships that plied the Rhine. Even in Germany, who would search for a Jew among longshoremen? "I ate *traiff*," Max confessed disgustedly, and I think he meant "eel" by the Yiddish word that means "filth" but translates to "unkosher." Crossing borders? "At night," he said. "There's always a place," but there was more to that than stealth. Max rubbed his callused fingers together in the universal sign for bribery.

In Brussels, Max opened his first coat factory. In explaining how a man goes into business, he illustrated the Spirit of Capitalism more succinctly than any student of Karl Marx. "You put your ass on a chair," he said, "and you do your work. But you eat less; pull in your belt. You understand this?" I nodded. "*Gut*. With the money you save, you buy another chair and hire some *schmuck* to sit in that. He does the same as you, but because you gave him the chair, you make more." Land, labor and capital? Theory of excess value-add? Max could have taught economics at Harvard.

He'd learned the needle trades from his father, but Max had the knack of taking any garment apart one stitch at a time to discover how the cloth had been cut. Cheaper materials, maybe a less elaborate collar and belt—he'd make a knockoff and undercut his competitors. His Belgian factory prospered, but the tale Allen, Minnie and Helena knew and loved was that of the woman who fired a revolver while pursuing Max through the streets of Brussels. I asked about it. He waved his hand. We were men of the world together. "*Ach.* What's to tell? She was *meshuggah.* There was a woman and then there was another woman." I was not smart enough to ask if Max had been married to either, a detail for which I am sure Minnie hungered. It was wonderful enough to learn that this bent-over man with gnarled fingers and the diamond pinky ring whose every day but Saturday began before dawn sitting on a high stool at a factory workbench with very sweet coffee in a blue cardboard cup and a cheese danish on wax paper had been a desperado.

Max made sufficient francs to finance more than a few Jewish refugees from Germany. He was fond of telling the story of the man he hid in his factory. Allen liked the story so much, he made it his own and never allowed his father to finish the tale. Max awakened to see the guy using his toothbrush, but Max said nothing. Later, in full sight of his guest, Max dropped his pants, squatted, and with his toothbrush cleaned his ass, inquiring of his guest if they used such hygienic instruments in the land he had come from.

When the *blitz* swept across Belgium, Max fled.

He fought with the Free French near the Swiss border, heading south until he bought his way into the hold of a tuna boat. It sailed from Marseilles. West of Gibraltar, in mid-Atlantic, Max transferred to a Canadian vessel.

The details grew foggy after that. Maybe he was fatigued by our sessions. There were always more officials to bribe, another border to cross at night, gold pieces sewn into the lining of his jacket. By WW II's end, he was out of Toronto and on the lower eastside of Manhattan where he sustained himself on a diet of rice and bananas, a fruit he'd never seen in Europe. He played Poker with the racketeers who ran the pressers union, the truckers union, the garment union. His credit with the shylocks was good. They took twenty-five percent, but no self-respecting *goyische* bank would finance the needle trades—far too risky. "Without the mob, we had no business," Max explained.

By the time Max's son the lawyer could help him with the process, when Max applied for citizenship in his 70s, he did not know an iota of American history. Lincoln was on the five; Washington on the one. Anything more was far beyond his American experience. "I pay my taxes for t'irty years and I employ one hundred people in my factory," Max said to the judge. The gavel slammed. On the spot, Max was pronounced a citizen. We had a party—cake and whiskey, the same as for a *bris*.

Max and Minnie followed their children the Americans and retired to Tucson, to be closer to their granddaughter, Jessica. It is in the way of things, of course, that Helena and I divorced before I finished graduate school, and Jessica soon after joined me in Iowa.

Less able to help themselves as they grew older, Max and Minnie's son warehoused them into a filthy home for the elderly in Miami. That proved so awful, they relocated again, shuttling back to their daughter in Tucson. Minnie, the young socialist whose father knew Freud, put her hand to her forehead and died of a stroke. Max, who evaded starvation and Nazis and ran through the streets of Brussels being shot at by a jilted lover, died in the deserts of the American Southwest, as well. As Helena tells it, he was sitting in a chair, mostly blind and unaware, and she went out of the room. When she came back, Max was gone.

David and Muriel

I don't care if you are a farmer's son in Wisconsin mired in mud to your hips, no one is more rooted to a place than a Brooklyn boy to his block. When I was 11, I attended junior high school and made my first friends who did not live in my neighborhood. My world expanded.

The apartment building in which I lived fronted Ocean Parkway, a borough-spanning boulevard designed by the Olmstead brothers, the same geniuses who'd designed Central and Prospect Parks. The street had a bridal path, over-arching oak and willow trees, benches and a paved bicycle path. One Saturday, after riding a bus for 20 minutes to Brighton Beach, a darker, more densely populated neighborhood huddled under the tracks of an elevated train, I visited my new friend, Eddie. As his mother served us sandwiches, the sleeve of her housecoat rode up to reveal the blue digits tattooed on her forearm. I had no idea what I had seen, but I sensed this was nothing to ask her about. Later, though, sitting on the brick stoop in front of Eddie's building, he filled me in on what he knew of Hitler's death camps and the Nazi passion for impeccable records.

That may be the first time I needed to brag that I was a third generation American. It kept Eddie's tales of horror at arm's length. Our family's safe superiority was a fact my mother drilled into her three children. We took pride in it. As Americans first and foremost, by birthright we were exempt from the hatred and death that had stalked European Jewry, a group my mother dismissed with a word she could spit, *mockey*. It meant any despicable Jew who spoke with an accent, the kind of Jews that made life more difficult for the Jews like herself. We were Yankees. Her grandmother was British, a woman who at 4 o'clock each day took high tea. The Jews of Eastern Europe—they were not like us.

The closest the Old World came to touching me directly was my father's father, Louis, a man who fled Austria rather than serve fifteen years in the army of the Emperor Franz Joseph. That's Eastern Europe, of course, and so our mother's self-aggrandizing distinctions did not strictly make sense for her children, but all three of us learned early to live with Muriel's contradictions. Louis the draft-dodger died when I was a child. Both of my grandmothers were buried before my birth. My mother's father, Lewis, lived with her sister and my father's brother, and that situation requires some explanation.

My father, David, married my mother, Muriel. David's older brother, Seymour, married Muriel's younger sister, Harriet. You might think that two brothers married to two sisters would forge family bonds of iron, but, in fact, the two couples did not speak for forty years.

There is no short version of the family history that created estrangement so powerful. It subsumed two score years of births, deaths, *bar mitzvahs* and marriages. My older brother and sister have no insights I do not. I can speculate, though.

When my father's mother died as a young woman, my father was summoned home from William and Mary where he had been on a football scholarship. His father and his older brother needed him to keep house. Born in 1912, a Jewboy in the Bronx, my Dad was rough and tough enough to play fullback, first at DeWitt Clinton High School and then at a college in Virginia. To be sure, that is not the chess team, so it must have been humiliating to have been summoned home to do woman's work. My father's childhood friends were Irish, and his three children knew by heart all his tales of brawls and speakeasies, but my father was a good son, obedient to his Old World father's wishes: he sacrificed his future to ensure that there would be a doctor in the family, his brother, Seymour, already in medical school. David pumped gas and kept house; his brother studied anatomy and physiology. No doubt, there was some understanding that Seymour in return would take care of his younger brother, David, forever.

You don't need details to know how that story ends, but there is the peculiar wrinkle that Seymour married Muriel's younger sister, Harriet. The competition between the two families was intense, and by most ordinary measures my mother and father could not compete. A physician simply makes a better living than a house painter, which is how my father supported his family, running the W&M Painting Company, named for his alma mater of eighteen months. My father and mother raised three children in a two-bedroom apartment; my aunt and uncle raised two children in a two-story brick house. The residences were three blocks and a universe apart.

So my parents' lives were a never-ending competition on a tilted playing field. As a defense against the always threatening world, they categorized everyone they knew in one of two ways: the first being a small group deemed "harmless," the second being all the rest. There was no category called "friends." They enjoyed two victories in their lives, and they relished both so much that the telling and retelling was ongoing.

The first victory came when I was barely old enough to be aware of it: my uncle dragged my father into court, but my father won a summary judgment that forced my uncle to pay more of the upkeep for their dying father. The judge was scandalized by the doctor's greed.

The second victory was more lasting, and that was the unequivocal success of Muriel and David's three children. We had no choice to do anything but succeed. My older brother, Harvey, is a physician. My sister, Toby, married well and has three fine daughters, and while that might not be the emblem of success for post-*Ms. Magazine* women, by my mother's and sister's lights, Toby did just fine, thank you very much. As for me, the spooky-smart youngest who seemed hell-bent on pissing away his abilities, after a lifetime of verbal abuse about what a dreamer and *putz* I was, once my second collection of fiction was published, my mother took pleasure in explaining to her retirement community neighbors how even in the cradle, I had such sharp, observant eyes that she knew I was destined to be a writer.

When it came to Jewish identity, the wave of self-awareness that swept American Jewry after WW II seems to have passed my parents by. The State of Israel is about two months older than I am, but my parents were not about to fight those distant battles when they were doing all they could struggling to remain on par in the war with their siblings. I don't recall collecting money for any tree-planting organizations. We sponsored no refugees. What for? No one we knew was in Israel, and if they had been, they'd get what they deserved for going to such a stupid place.

Nevertheless, my sense of Jewishness was strong because in my mother's unending battle with the wider world, Jewishness—not the faith, but the identity—was a potent weapon that bolstered her frail sense of social position. Muriel indoctrinated me with considerable ethnic pride via mass culture, the sole source for most of what she knew. A bright woman, she'd finished high school, but that was the end of her formal education. She read few books. What she knew of biblical history she learned from Cecil B. deMille. In her head lived a vast storehouse of world personalities who were Jewish, a list she readily shared with her children whenever our TV flickered into life. Milton Berle, of course. Jack Benny. George Burns. Jerry Lewis. Later, Barbra Streisand. By my mother's lights, every successful or wealthy American was probably Jewish. This list amazingly included Frank Sinatra, though if pressed she would admit that Sinatra might be Italian, partly.

I came of age believing there was more than one kind of Jew in the world. First, there was the kind that was pursued, captured and gassed, probably because of some defect in their make-up that could be traced to odd accents and devotion to arcane rituals. Second, there was our kind of Jew, Americans who happened to eat bagels and because of a cultural imperative to achieve invented the 20th century. Marx, Freud, and Einstein were a potent troika about which my mother knew little, but she was aware of their importance. She relished the irony that Irving Berlin, a Jew, wrote America's best loved Christmas and Easter ballads, as well as what should have been the national anthem, and her children at some level were all made aware that great fortunes accrued by the Guggenheims, Sulzbergers, and Bronfmans were partly turned to public good. That the Bronfmans were Canadian was a mere technicality. My mother's darlings were the gang that created the American Dream Factory, Goldwyn, Fox, Mayer, and the Warner brothers, all Jews like us, the Jews that would prevail.

So my family was Jewish, but only as a kind of reaction formation to the Gentile world. Our identification as Jews did not go as far as acknowledging community with victims, and we tacitly blamed victims for their victimization, a common psychological tactic to create an illusion of separation and—because the world for Jews is what it is—safety. The displaced beggars who inconveniently flooded the world shortly before I was born were nothing but *mockeys*, and the notion of "family" in our house was a schism so deep that when we buried my father, my mother was astonished to see my uncle, Seymour. "What the hell are you doing here?" she asked from her wheelchair across the open grave, and when Seymour answered from his wheelchair, "He was my brother!" Muriel waved her hand dismissively.

My parents both lived into their early 80s, my mother winning her family's longevity race. There must be some benefit to a lifetime of spleen, because though she was the oldest of three children, she buried her younger brother and sister, as well as outliving her husband and his older brother. Muriel died in her sleep, a fact I take as the sign of God's compassion.

Perry and Helena

Helena and I were 21 when we married, refugees desperate to flee our families. Today, we'd have simply moved out and shared an apartment, but in that time and place, such willful independence was a nonstarter, even for self-styled rebels.

At our wedding, I wore a rented tuxedo. Helena wore a satin white wedding gown. At 96 pounds with auburn hair to the small of her back, crowned by a Spanish mantilla, she was gorgeous. It is a measure of who we were and when we were that in March of 1970 we had instructed our wedding band to play no music from *Fiddler on the Roof* nor any *horas*, the traditional Jewish circle dance. No wedding singer would warble her way through "Sunrise, Sunset" while we sat, humiliated, squirming at such naked *yiddischekeit*. But someone slipped the band $20, and so the musicians ignored the snot-nosed kids who were not paying them and played a *hora* anyway. We left the party two hours before it ended, presumably because we were anxious to be alone. In fact, we could not endure the lavish event arranged by Helena's parents. After a sexless night, we flew to the Playboy Club and Resort in fabulous fun-filled Ocho Rios, Jamaica. For a week, large-breasted women poised on three-inch stiletto heels in bunny outfits and black fishnet stockings bent their knees to serve us rum drinks. We hated cameras; there are no photos of our honeymoon. Helena badly cut a toe while making the mandatory tourist climb up Dunn's River Falls. Her blood ran in streamers in the waters flowing over the rocks. I read a British paperback edition of *The Godfather*—tyres and lorries and mayhem. After eight days of enjoying the Honeymoon Package, we flew back to our new apartment chosen for its proximity to a Brooklyn elevated train station and the fact that the apartment had a second small bedroom where, I imagined, I'd write. We settled in for what was supposed to be the rest of our lives.

Helena and I arrived at our denial of our Jewish identities from opposite ends of the spectrum that spanned the Jewish experience in post-war America. While Helena's parents worked to forget what was unforgettable, my parents denied what was undeniable. Helena's parents had survived unspeakable horror and so kept their children ignorant of their history; my parents reveled in a highly selective history, one where Jews were masters of the universe, powerful icons of success. Helena's parents in the New World created synthetic families for which the simple fact of proximity at birth was reason enough to call someone "uncle"; my parents engaged in a 40-year family schism that persisted to the grave.

Even a poor student of the first half of the 20th century will recognize that Helena's and my choice to define ourselves as American was the same delusion that enabled the eradication of European Jewry. The appearance of assimilation was so seductive that the advent of genocide was discounted by Hitler's victims, making them passive collaborators in the events that eventually loaded them onto boarded, airless cattle cars that lurched to a halt at a railroad spur in Auschwitz. Thousands fled, but millions dismissed the Evil about to engulf them, equating self-imposed blindness with safety. They said, *We are Germans* or *We are French* or *We are Italians* or *We are Poles*. They said this with confidence to their Gentile neighbors. They said this to assure each other. They continued to say this even as their German, French, Italian and Polish neighbors starved, beat, stripped and herded them into showers that washed naked men, women, and children in deadly fumes of Zyklon-B.

At a time less steeped in blood but no less delusional, Helena and I chose to believe our identity was a matter of personal choice, not history. *We are Americans*, we said, fully expecting that personal reinvention, self-actualization and self-determination were our rights as citizens. *We are Americans*, we said, believing that the society that prides itself on mobility and change would nurture and welcome us. *We are Americans*, we said, lustily singing songs Pete Seeger or Woody Guthrie might play, folk music and ballads about whalers, railroaders, Kentucky coal miners and cowboys, vocations seldom associated with any breathing Yid.

The daughter of a Polish tailor and the son of a Bronx housepainter, we had been intoxicated with Kerouac and all that promise of distance and open space. If the essential American idea is that identity is a choice, the first corollary is that movement is the manifestation of that choice. That principle explains everything from America's devotion to gas-guzzling autos to why a Senator from Tennessee named Crockett died in Texas. In America, one-third of the population identifies itself as "born again." Why not? A fresh start is an American birthright. Ask the pioneers. Ask any gaggle of Watergate felons.

But in the West, far from the ethnic constraints of our east coast origins, Helena and I confronted the irrevocable differences of our Jewishness. The habits and convictions we believed we were free to shed could not be dropped. Subtle reminders of our differences arose everywhere.

Graduate school in Arizona had an air of unreality for me, a Jew from the East. I made friends with people whose greatest ambitions were to remain graduate students forever. As smart and as clever as any people I'd ever known, I found my goodwill sullied by contempt for men who wanted to read, smoke dope, frequently form and break sexual liaisons, and gave little thought to competing in the Great Game of Life, the perpetual competition for which my parents had prepared me. One close friend explained that as long as he could stay attached to the University teat, he was omitting years of fruitless labor that lay between him and that promised life of tennis and golf. He planned never to marry; he wanted no children.

My mother and father had a word for lotus-eaters: *Bums.*

It was work for me to lay aside my prejudice. These were good, kind, smart people; just not like Helena and me.

Other reminders of our differences arose in Arizona. Helena and I owned a condo in the foothills to the west of Tucson, and when we invited our new friends to join us for a barbecue in our backyard, three of my classmates showed up wearing shirts and ties, assuming that was what the Jewish New Yorkers would expect. They were startled, if relieved, to find me barefoot and in frayed denim cutoffs. My friends tolerated my strangeness, and several were fond of the guy who talked too much but could be funny as all get out, even if he did have a smidgen more ambition than was seemly and played a game of chess a shade too ruthless.

Beyond Arizona, out in America, Helena and I found constant reminders of our difference: the oddness of the Baby Jesus and crèche at the town hall, a tax-funded display for which our friends could not fathom our objections; radio stations that read gospel 24 hours per day as a public service; office Christmas parties where well-meaning colleagues propose a toast reminding all present of "the real meaning of Christmas," by which they mean God giving His only Son to die for the sins of everyone in the room, including the heathens graciously admitted to their midst; Mormons at the front door that ask, "Are you Christian?"; friends who earnestly invite us to church because they value the social aspect of community worship and are slightly wounded when we decline; people who spread mayonnaise on deli meat sandwiches or, only slightly less barbaric, prefer light mustard; a basket of Easter goodies given in good will, for our daughter's sake; acquaintances who confess they never ate bagels as children and now that they are adults still cannot imagine eating fish at breakfast. They have no idea what a bialy might be. They call lox "smoked salmon" and ask earnest questions about customs, unaware how their use of the word "Jew" slides from being a reference to religion, to a nationality, and, most odiously, a reference to race.

We should have listened to the Rolling Stones more carefully:

Oh, a storm is threat'ning
My very life today
If I don't get some shelter
Oh yeah, I'm gonna fade away.

The strains of life in the West proved to be too much for Helena and me. Two years after first breathing the thinner desert air, Helena felt the need to become wholly someone else. She was suffocating. In the two months after a judge dissolved our union, she remarried, severing herself from not only me, but, eventually, her daughter as well.

Neither amputation wholly succeeded. Years later, the futility of making a clean break with her heritage still plagued her. Thirty years after our union and twenty years after our separation, on a day when she suffers a minor marital spat with her Gentile husband, in her bewilderment she picks up the phone and calls me. "What is it with *goyim* and Jews?"

I hear her exasperation. Whom else can she ask? You can't make new old friends.

As I swing through middle age, Yiddish phrases—mostly learned from Helena's parents—pepper my speech. Though I never attend services, as a matter of pride I tell my employers in advance I will be out on Rosh Hashanah and Yom Kippur; the High Holy Days may not be celebratory events, but I want the people around me to respect that I am a Jew.

One sparkling morning, my second wife, the *shiksa*, reveals she is no longer heterosexual. We part with reluctance and regret. An American, she had the option to start anew; a Jew I go forward with the sole life I have. I've learned that the most American of ideas, the option for rebirth, for a Jew is absurd.

There is no being born-again, no rebirth by baptism. There is no confession. There is no deathbed absolution. For a Jew, suffering has no redemptive value; it is just suffering. For a Jew, identity is a persistent weight that cannot be shed for a glorious sprint to a new finish. In a land where people believe they can seize, build, or demand whatever identity they wish, being a Jew remains as immutable as skin tone. Being a Jew is not a matter of practice, it is a matter of essence. There is no shelter.

Helena and I would have become *goyim*, but they would not have us. As Jews, we know History intimately. We might change our name, we might attend a Unitarian Church, we might marry Gentiles, we might do whatever we wish to swim in the mainstream.

But as Jews, we can never relinquish the certainty that if in some nightmare future the Gestapo rises once more, exactly as they did in the culture of Beethoven, Schiller and Kant, our neighbors will lift their hands and point.

There, there is the Jew.

Hey Joe
The Jimi Hendrix Experience

In Sullivan County, New York, the languid turns of Route 17 lie gently on the lush Catskill hills, but in our headlamps on this moonless August night, at 135 mph the turns come up so fast that the road appears no more than an unraveling ribbon of gnarled concrete. It's 1968, and sanity is in short supply. Newark and Detroit burned a summer ago. Flag-draped black vinyl body bags stack like cordwood on landing docks and in airplane hangars, so many American dead in the Tet offensive that in February no less a figure than Walter Cronkite pronounces the war in Vietnam unwinnable. Martin Luther King is shot dead in April, Parisian students riot in May, Robert Kennedy is shot dead in June, and the Democratic National Convention will in a week fill the streets of Chicago with teargas, homicidal cops, and the blood of hippies. We race on Mr. Toad's Wild Ride, but some fool has stolen the guardrails. We are spinning out of control.

I figure that the pine tree that will end my life waits hidden in the wall of darkness beyond the bug-spattered windshield of Mike's MGB Coupe, a car dubbed Eloise. We'll swerve to avoid a deer or some such foolishness, and we'll die in the night. "Fuck deer," Mike says, "Eloise slides right under any fucking deer."

Eloise skids around the worst of the turns, so low to the ground Mike boasts he can drag his knuckles if he dares to hang an arm out the window. More casual than Junior Johnson hisself running 'shine through the North Carolina piney woods, Mike steers with his left wrist while he shifts with his right hand. Mike's contraband of choice is the joint he smokes, which he claims helps focus his attention. He also claims that Eloise has a soul that better responds to the road when Hendrix is on the 8-track. With two six-inch speakers cranked to max mounted in the hardtop roof just behind our ears, the top line of "Hey Joe" is an icicle spiked through my ear; the bass line and drums rumble just south of my belly. The voices mixed below the melody are a ghostly choir sweetly singing about jealousy, betrayal, murder, and flight. On this same tape, we've got "Manic Depression," "Purple Haze," and "Foxy Lady." An epoch has passed in the four years since the Fab Four in sharply creased suits and thin ties charmed us with, "I Want to Hold Your Hand." America has descended from Love to twitching psychosis.

Eloise's sealed windows trap smoke and sound. The car balks and wobbles at these speeds if we dare crack a window and break the aerodynamic design, a green artillery shell on chrome-spoke wheels. The dope gives me only a light contact high; my nose is more numbed by the aroma emanating from the grease-stained brown paper bag in my grasp that contains two still hot-to-the-touch roast pork and garlic-bread sandwiches, each twelve inches long and wrapped in twisted aluminum foil. The sandwiches reek like sewage, but when God Himself wants comfort food, He appears at Jerry and Lil's in Parksville, New York, and orders one to go, double-stuffed.

No such unkosher delicacy is to be found at the Jewish summer camp where we are counselors, so this food-run to score a late night nosh is worth any and all risk, down to and including some ambitious state trooper discovering the half-kilo stash wedged behind Eloise's spare tire. In Texas in 1968, that's enough weight to get us thirty years of hard time, but in more enlightened New York Mike might get twenty and me a mere five. "Not to worry," Mike reassures me. "The fucker will have to catch us first." His hands abandon the quivering steering wheel to pass the joint from left to right to me, but I turn down his third offer of a hit. The odometer spins like a slot machine. When he downshifts for the unpaved one-lane rutted road that climbs the mountainside to camp, Eloise's bald Michelins spit clods of dirt that clatter like rounds from a Gatling gun in the wheel well. Mike roars over Hendrix, "Three miles! Five minutes! We're a lock! Fuck curfew! We're golden!"

In the crawlspace behind Eloise's two leather bucket seats, as if she were in her own warm bed, sleeps my girlfriend, Helena. Bone-skinny, all elbows, knees, and long hair, Helena looks like a geometry problem that has been folded up and put away to be solved at some future date. She is not hung over. She is not drunk. Except for a mild buzz no greater than mine, she's far from stoned. It has just been a long day beneath the sun, she is tired, and she is not one to squander a chance to cop a few Z's.

Eloise growls, the car lurches forward, and I realize that if I live I will have to marry her. In a world gone mad, what are the chances I will find another girl for whom garlic, Hendrix, speed, a felony drug rap, and imminent death pose no obstacle to a quick nap?

Two years earlier, for my second semester of required French, I enrolled a second time in Professor Spagnoli's class. No one fails Spagnoli's class. It's a political thing. A young man who flunks out of college loses his student status, and that ends his draft deferment. Spangnoli is a frail old man with bright brown eyes who does not care to condemn young men to violent death in jungle mud because they do not grasp the niceties of the subjunctive *imparfait* for the second conjugation verb, *savoir*. My first college semester, my test average is a dismal 57. French, Pig Latin, and Urdu are all the same to me, but Spagnoli awards me a D, striking his blow against the empire, no small gesture at a time when his sanctimonious colleagues utter pieties about the integrity of the academic community. Shall mere politics corrupt scholastic standards? *Fie on it!* Better to send youth into free-fire zones! Understand, Spagnoli's academic generosity takes more courage than it may seem. The professor grimaces when he sees me reappear for a new, more advanced semester, but he greets me with an impish, conspiratorial smile.

A girl comes into the room, slightly tardy. On that murky, gray January day in Brooklyn, snow fine as ash falls in fitful bursts from clouds the color of an old bruise. Her enormous, impenetrably dark wraparound sunglasses cover whatever part of her face remains unhidden by her full hair, some of which is gathered by a leather clip and cascades to the small of her back. She wears a brown and black hound's tooth peacoat, the collar raised, her hands closed to fists deep in the chest-high pockets. She passes where I sit in my habitual seat near a classroom's rear door, the fastest getaway at dismissal. While Spagnoli rattles on about the dedication we will need to explore the pleasures and challenges of Racine and Moliere, knowing she must be stoned, I whisper to her, "Wow, sure is bright out. I wish I wore my shades."

She bends forward, pushes some hair aside, and whispers, "Fuck you, prick," before she heads for a desk at the far side of the room.

I am in Brooklyn College's Scholar's Program, which except for a few required courses like French means I am engaged in a lot of independent study under the loose supervision of a few indulgent professors. The program is a funded Cold War strategy to cultivate the geniuses who will beat the Russians. We have catching up to do. Though the commies are first into space, John Kennedy has set us on course to beat the Reds to the Moon. No one gives a rat's ass about French, but since I am a Math major and Physics minor who might create more lethal ICBMs or will design laser weapons to zap death onto America's enemies from orbit, I am allowed to hang out in an exclusive lounge where someone gifted at the piano is always playing Moonlight Sonata.

The Program proves socially isolating, so when during a fall membership drive at an interview I correctly differentiate between a dildo and a phallic symbol, I am invited to join Kingsley House, a social club. Think *fraternity* with no ritual or national organization. We field intramural teams and we have parties. In a smoky room filled with loud music and sweating undergraduates, I meet for the second time the skinny girl in shades who will become my wife for twelve years and bear my only child.

"You're the asshole from Spagnoli's class," she says.

"D minus," I say.

Her, too.

Her rat-brown Rambler takes us to a diner. It's all chrome, glass, and black Formica counters arranged to seem like a railroad car. We glom French Toast, smoke cigarettes, and drink coffee in a bench-seat booth. A quarter buys three tunes off the chrome jukebox. We slouch low, our feet propped up on the seat opposite. Helena's finger traces her initials through the condensation on the window glass. I pick at the duct tape that seals a wound in the red leatherette near my hip. The diner is open all night. The coffee refills are free and the waitress is amenable. We linger, and when my cigarettes are finished, we smoke Helena's, and when those are finished, rather than invest in separate packs, we compromise on a fresh pack of Parliaments, weaker than my Marlboros, stronger than her Kents. Parliaments become our brand.

Mostly we talk writers. Having aced Calculus after six weeks of independent study, the Math Department hopes it has a new star, but my secret is that I'd rather read a book than rotate a curve.

This is a time in my life when I cannot formulate a sentence without the word *fuck*, but Helena proves to be as foul-mouthed as I am. It's not so much a ballsy pose as it is the diction of Brooklyn. She likes e.e. cummings, a poet who is fucking amazing, but her recent discovery is *A Coney Island of the Mind*, poems by Lawrence Ferlinghetti, a book she picked up because of the title. Her copy of *Howl* is also used, bought for $.35 off a rack at a 4th Avenue book store. I've read the fucking poem. Up until this moment, I have never known anyone other than myself who might take the subway to wander among used bookstores in Lower Manhattan. We talk about the Strand, a place that in basements and sub-basements holds a labyrinth of floor-to-ceiling dusty bookracks, rickety ladders, and sales clerks who know everything worth knowing about everything ever written by anyone at any time in any place in any fucking language in the entire fucking world. I confess that I am in a smart-kids special program. This doesn't put her off. She's interested. So I tell her I've just read something called *Growing Up Absurd* by Paul Goodman, a book I've come to after Alan Watts' *Psychotherapy, East and West*, which came after *Siddhartha* and *Steppenwolf*. My high school English teachers cultivated my habit: good books suggest more good books, and you follow the trail. I mention I want to be a writer. Instead of laughing, she tells me her favorite poem by Ferlinghetti. She says, "Constantly risking absurdity and death…something, something,

something." It's about how poets take risks like high wire walkers. Writers. Fuck, yeah, writers are okay.

As I compose this forty years later, the memory startles me. We were semi-articulate kids who unashamedly talked about ideas as if they were our own; we read serious books, even poetry, for pleasure. The stuff mattered. Helena was a skinny kid with horn-rimmed glasses; I needed to shave every three days or so, my upper lip not at all. We cared.

So we make a date. Helena will show me the whole poem. It turns out the poem defines my life for a long while. Still.

Good writing came with hard effort. I liked that. Writing attracted girls. I liked that, too. Writing is narcissistic—the writer's first leap is to believe he has something to say that other people need to hear. Yeah, well, here I am. Writing explained the world by narrative, and writing allowed my compulsive imagination to seek a world more sensible and more just than the world I knew.

Writers. Fuck, yeah, writers are okay.

Months later, we have sex. Such events move slower then. It is my first time. It is not hers, so to even the score and make myself feel better about myself I tell her she is not my first, either. The lie leeches toxins into my psyche; I never correct it. When things start out wrong, there is no fixing them, not without discovering a kind of courage forever beyond my reach.

So when at 21 we marry for several complicated reasons, only one of which may be a kind of love, I begin to wonder: *What have I missed?* My sense of loss weighs on me. I know; I know. My resentment is not a rational thing. We are long past rational.

Helena has done nothing wrong; I can't forgive her.

Noxious seeds take root in her mind, too. Helena's favorite song when we meet is Bob Dylan's "Tom Thumb's Blues" because, while listening to Dylan, she and a girlfriend smoke dope in her basement and exhale onto a gerbil. The stoner-rodent runs wildly on its wheel, reducing both girls to helpless giggles. Now, I never smoked more than two joints with Helena or anyone else, for that matter. I will sit in a room or car with anyone who smokes weed, but no tokes over the line is just fine for me. But in divorce counseling fourteen years later, I learn my attitudes towards marijuana suffocate Helena's lifestyle. I over-control her life. I have denied her self-determination. When she ticks off my transgressions on the fingers of her hand, her sense of guilt for smoking marijuana is number three, close behind my having urged her to accept a job that doubled her salary in our second year of marriage, a defect second only to how well I have gotten along with her parents. I am not her ally. Her resentment is not a rational thing. We are long past rational.

I've done nothing wrong; she cannot forgive me.

To Hell with Hendrix. Whole lifetimes are available for regret, revenge, and recrimination; let celebration have its season.

In Brooklyn, where boys pick up billiards as readily as Hoosiers dribble basketballs, Helena often watched me chalk up at Jackie Cannon's, a dingy poolroom in a basement on Flatbush Avenue. In her worn jeans, smoking Parliaments, for long afternoons into early evening and late at night, she sat on one of those high wooden chairs. Cannon, a lean, middle-aged Irishman with freckles and a full head of red hair, bought her soft drinks and gave her quarters to feed the jukebox. Helena was partial to "Eight Miles High," the Byrds song by Roger McGuinn and David Crosby. While I applied blue chalk delicate as lipstick to a cue and peered over green felt to line up a shot, she and Cannon talked politics or evaluated the day's racing card.

Helena knew the horses as well as anyone. Better. Our fathers were horseplayers, though neither was much of a gambler. Max owned a coat factory. Saturdays, after morning prayers at *shul*, still in his suit and tie, he drove to wherever the breed was being improved in New York City, Aqueduct or Belmont. He paid a few extra dollars to sit in the Clubhouse with owners and trainers. My father, on the other hand, on weekdays when he had no work, dressed in his white overalls so my mother had no clue where he'd been, went to the races to bet small amounts he could not afford to lose on long-shots. Along with hundreds of other railbirds in the general admission Grandstand, for two bucks he bought a few minutes of hope—not altogether a bad deal, when you think about it.

Go find an 18-year old girl today who knows that decent time for a $25,000 claimer is 1:11 for six furlongs. Helena knew the fixed weight carried by horses in the Kentucky Derby, the distance of every race in the Triple Crown, and that in 1948, the year of our birth, Citation won all three races under Eddie Arcaro, the jockey known as "Banana Nose." We are not talking about some suburban kid in jodhpurs and a black helmet on an English saddle; the only horse Helena ever mounted was on a merry-go-round, and if she had not been strapped on, she'd have fallen off. She knew that animals not for eating were for betting.

We are still students when at the races I loan her this absurd blue madras porkpie rain hat, but the moment she sweeps her hair up under it, exposing that regal neck, the hat becomes hers, rain or shine. Our friend Eddie calls her Leo Gorcey when she does that, but no one thinks she looks like the lead in the Dead End Kids; it is all in the pugnacious attitude. She has plenty of that.

When lying, rapacious, murderous bastards wage war and run your country in pursuit of profit and power, being profane is a virtue.

Slouched on a wooden Grandstand seat, the hat drawn low over her eyes, Helena seems to sit on her neck. Her shoulders are lower than her bony hips, her ass in the air with her weight on her knobby spine, the soles of her unpolished penny loafers braced against the slats of the seatback in front of her. She studies her copy of the *Daily Racing Form*, properly folded into a long column, her dark eyes moving over the tiny print as intently as she reads Turgenev, Lermontov, or Gogol, Russian writers she absorbs as quickly as other people read Mickey Spillane. As the call to the colors sounds—*riders up!*—the horses slowly parade to the gate. With ten minutes left to place a wager, her stubby grease pencil poised over her program, Helena pushes back her hat, and peers up at me from under those dark, dark brows to ask, "Who do you like?"

This will sound like we should have been in Gambler's Anonymous, but Helena was a very serious cardplayer. She was proud of being "one of the guys." This is before "feminism" was an ism. She adored being told she played Poker as well as a man. And she did. Better, mostly. She carried her bulky wallet in her frayed back pocket because with a menstrual cycle that was at best a sometimes thing, other than a hairbrush, why would she know the uses of a purse?

One night at Kingsley House, we yield to group insanity and deal Acey-Deucey. Most card games, you play against the other players, but in Acey-Deucey you play against the pot. Everyone puts up a dollar or two. The pack is shuffled, two cards are turned face up to each player in turn, and the player bets any amount up to the whole pot that the next card will numerically fall between the first two. Since a tie is a negative result, some hands are simply unwinnable. No one can draw a third card between a five and a six, for example, but a player still must toss in the minimum bet. So the game can go on forever; there's a player who never gets tired—the pot. If anyone decides to go home—even if everybody decides to go home—whose money is that piled in the middle of the table? How should it be divided? Better to play until someone takes it all.

That night the cards are treacherous. Someone

might be dealt a king and a four, bet five dollars on what seemed an easy win, and the next card comes up a three. It was uncanny. We are at first giddy with how the odds are beating us, but then we become grim. As we go through the pack, reshuffle, and go through it again, three separate times a player dealt the best possible hand, ace-deuce, calls "Pot," a wager that will end the game, and three separate times the player loses to an ace or deuce. Ties are a loss. The odds against this are astronomical. Nevertheless, the pot doubles, redoubles, and doubles again. Lots of smoke. Lots of quiet. Nothing more than the snap of the cards. The pot is cleaning us out.

Doug deals Helena a king and a three. She says, "Pot," reflexively, doesn't even think to count how much money that is to see if she can afford to lose. That was her way; Helena knows a gambler must take her chances when they come. No gambler gambles for long with scared money.

But Irwin says, "Nothing doing." Doug agrees. Irwin and his family live two blocks from Helena in an apartment over his mother's store. She sells "foundation garments" to Helena's mother. Doug had gone to junior high with Helena, and he worked as the soda jerk in the candy store down the street from her house. He knows her family well enough to call Helena's mother "Minnie" and Minnie calls him "Dougie," but Dougie does not snap the next card over. Cigarette ashes fall to his chest as he says to Helena, "Where's your money?"

Helena laughs. Doug has to be kidding. Here is a guy who makes her egg creams and forgets to take her money off the counter at his job. "I'll write you an I.O.U.," she says.

Doug looks to Irwin. "Nothing doing," Irwin repeats, and adds, "Cash only."

If they can make Helena bet less than the pot's total, then they preserve their hope to recoup their losses. The other players agree. I keep my mouth shut. There's not much I can say; if Helena's boyfriend objects, who will be surprised?

The moment is causing Helena some pain. Cold cash or bet less. They count on intimidating the girl in their midst. One-hundred and twelve dollars is at stake.

"All right," she says. "I'll get it."

Her chair scrapes the floor as she pushes back from the table. She stands, tells me to watch the fucking cards, swings on her peacoat, and charges down the steps and out the door. We hear her car engine start. This is near two o'clock in the morning.

Twenty-five minutes later, she returns with six twenty-dollar bills in her fist. Her face is flushed, her hair the usual mess half over her eyes, her coat collar raised around her ears as a defense from the chilled night, the final stub of a cigarette between her thumb and index finger. Her dark eyes are hard as marbles, and from that I know she has gone to her father, awakened him, and he has loaned her the money.

Years spent proving to herself and the world that she is not "Daddy's little girl" and now having to ask Max for money must have cost her, but, then again, Max would bankroll a good Poker hand for a total stranger faster than he would invest in 100 bolts of next season's fabric.

Helena never sits. She stubs her cigarette into an overflowing ashtray, slaps the bills down on the table and spits the word, "Pot."

Nine of diamonds.

Helena doesn't whoop or smile. Nothing. Like she expected it, is entitled, knew it all along, and is super-pissed with us for requiring her to demonstrate what so plainly was obvious. She is destined to win. She stuffs big fistfuls of crumpled money, mostly ones and fives, into her coat pockets. And then she leaves us to stare stupidly at each other.

Yeah, you could say Helena played cards.

Helena is no athlete. Not that she isn't game; she participates in all manner of co-ed sports when we are students, but toss a ball into the air, and if she does not trip over her own feet, Helena will run in tiny circles until the ball drops to the ground somewhere in her vicinity.

She yearns most for tennis. Maybe the good looks of the Aussie amateurs who dominate the game first attracted her, but she learns to appreciate serve, volley and the charge to net of the power game. We become regulars at the earliest rounds of the annual Forest Hills Tennis Tournament, today's US Open. The humidity in Queens in early September is tropical, and since her thick hair traps heat, she wears a yellow terrycloth hat. Her sundress is a green and white pair of culottes, her thin legs brown with sun, her eyes hidden by the same thick sunglasses in which I first see her. Helena buys a printed copy of the brackets and precisely pencils in winners and losers, noting the scores on days we cannot attend by checking results in *The New York Times*. She keeps these score sheets for years; she may still have them.

A spectator can walk on the grass between courts in those days, eating chilled strawberries and yogurt or sipping a flute of champagne, close enough to hear Emerson and Newcombe and Laver and Roche curse, spit, and swear at each other, the umpires and themselves. Tennis is not yet a cash machine requiring players to be walking billboards with product names on every garment or piece of equipment they use, but is a sport for pretty-boy athletes who wear white, for royalty who clap, for rich people who pay club dues, and for kids who attended summer camp, kids like me. "Tennis anyone?" is the punch line to jokes about affectation. Amateurs can win no prize money; the players travel with, and seem genuinely to like, each other. Their camaraderie charms us as much as the play. Women's tennis is a mere sideshow. Those tall, handsome, tanned, lean men in tight whites with muscled legs and arms chat up Helena, a young woman they understandably mistake for the heiress to a fortune.

But being an enthusiastic spectator is insufficient. Her wrists are so thin, she cannot manage to hold a racket. Still, she wants to do something, anything physical. So since she never learned to ride a bike, for her birthday one year I buy us a tandem.

The thing weighs slightly less than a Mack truck.

The miracle lightweight alloys employed today do not then exist. A blacksmith may have hammered this bike into shape from salvaged wrought iron. It rides smooth as a Panzer tank. We tour the esplanade that circles Brooklyn along the Narrows, passing under the Verrazano Bridge, Staten Island a green cat's back rising in the haze across the water. At every slight rise, I stand to pedal, sweating like a Singapore rickshaw coulee. Helena swears she is pedaling as hard as she can; in fact, when I steal a look I see she sits behind me with her feet up on her useless handlebars. She smokes a cigarette, careful to exhale into the wind that carries the smoke behind us.

Picture that.

In a year when we run with the crowd of gay men we came to know through my sister's decorator, on another birthday, I gift Helena with a daylong session at Elizabeth Arden, the tony beauty salon in mid-Manhattan. Helena stalls for weeks before she makes the appointment and finally spends six hours behind the red door on Fifth Avenue. We all agree to meet at *La Champignon*.

Every eye in the place follows her as she arrives. Our gay friends are mute, a rare condition. This is post-Stonewall, pre-AIDS New York City, and such silence in this chattering crowd is rare. The word "stunning" can be literal.

Helena is 24. Her hair is lustrous, deep, even, and styled to sweep over one eye. She is a brunette Lauren Bacall with no Bogart in sight. Her brows are plucked perfectly, maybe the only day in her life she has more than one eyebrow. The makeup they've applied to so young a woman is slight—blush, lipstick, a hint of mascara, blue-eyeliner. Her skin is radiant. She wears a high-collared cream-colored taffeta blouse, sleeves to ruffled cuffs; her embroidered burgundy leather gaucho vest matches her miniskirt. The antique cameo near her throat has never looked this good. Her nails glisten with a rich polish that matches the color on her lips. Her knee-high 3-inch-heel boots click smartly as she strides across the restaurant's parquet oak floor. The ox-blood brown leather of her shoulder strap bag matches her boots. Barefoot, Helena is 5' 6" and weighs less than 100 pounds. What weight she has is in her chest. With those high cheekbones and dark brown eyes, she looks to me as though she should be wrapped in sable and bundled into a sled pulled by a troika of matched black horses, a silver cloud of breath at her lips, baying wolves in hot pursuit.

"I guess I look pretty good," she whispers to me while for the only time I can recall in our lives together, she waits for the restaurant host to draw back her chair.

We order her a Black Russian, naturally. She opens her purse and withdraws a crimson box of Balkan Sobraines, cigarettes rolled in black paper with gold filter tips. Our friends gush. When I hold my butane lighter to light her cigarette, she steadies my wrist with her two hands and her hair falls slightly forward to frame her face, golden in the glow of the flame.

No one thought to bring a camera. We are that unprepared.

Some night in 1968 or 1969, Helena and I double date with Steve and Carol, a couple who stay married for 35 years before cancer takes Carol. If you are lucky, you have such friends, people who knew you when and care about you now. That night the four of us go to a movie, or for coffee, or who knows what. No one is married yet. We are kids.

Steve guides his father's car through dark Brooklyn streets. Helena is first drop, then me. This is not geographically sensible, but it is a plan that will eventually leave Steve and Carol alone in the vehicle to find a dark street. I walk with Helena up the narrow concrete driveway to the side entrance of the two-family brick house where she lives with her parents and brother on the floor above a tenant I never see. We part. I walk back down the alley.

When I return to the car's backseat, Carol and Steve are stifling giggles. "What?" I ask as Steve pulls away. It's a cool night, but the windows are open. Night air flows over me.

"It's nothing," Steve says, and breaks up. Steve knows Helena since grade school.

Carol turns on the seat, rests her chin on the backrest and says to me, laughing, "What *is* it with you two? No one has ever seen you kiss."

My smile is involuntary. At parties, couples will dance close, they will neck on the couch, and everyone has in a dim room seen a guy's hand go under his girl's blouse. But not Helena and me. No. Public displays of affection are not for us.

I smile at Carol, unsure why her question is funny to her.

"What do you mean?" I say.

"Oh, Steve and I had a bet. He won." Carol laughs again and turns around on her seat.

"So what's funny?" I ask, and they laugh again.

My last year at college, I share a hotel room with Mark and two others. It's the three-day weekend when Brooklyn College's social organizations cart busloads of students to some bucolic hotel resort where we carouse and play volleyball. People get hurled into swimming pools. It's Spring Break.

Only commuters attend Brooklyn College. As a commuter's school, all-night bull sessions, the center of the educational experience for the hundreds of thousands of undergraduates who attend land grant universities or private colleges across the country, just don't happen for us. Student strikes close Harvard, Berkeley and Columbia. Bombs explode in Wisconsin. But at Brooklyn College, starting a revolution proves awkward; everyone at the sit-in must be home in time for dinner.

That night, we dress for cocktails, dinner, and a night of dancing, which means no more than pulling on fresh jeans and shrugging into dry shirts. That time, that place, that culture, none of us is more than 20, the drinking age is 18, and those of us not engaged are presumed to be dating the women we will marry. You will notice we do not room with our girlfriends or fiancés.

The four of us elbow for position at the mirror in a

room damp with shower steam. We are having our bull session. It is very satisfactory, more so for being rare. Ashtrays and Old-Fashioned glasses that hold melting ice, butts, and the residue of bourbon, scotch or rye, are scattered on every horizontal surface. We are partial to brown liquors. Beer is for peasants or baseball games. The room smells of Aqua Velva and Old Spice.

A towel draped over his hips, Mark lies otherwise naked, supine on a white bedspread, his hands laced at his neck. We went to the same high school. We were boys together and are not quite yet men. I once sat in his mother's kitchen and waited 45 minutes for Mark to eat a single hamburger. No bread. No ketchup. Everyone I knew would inhale the thing and be done, but Mark, who ran cross-country, was never known for speed but for patience. At the right moment, if he detected another runner who might falter, he made his move. His skin is fish-belly pale. He is slender. He studies hard. Years later, he will become the kind of attorney that never litigates. He says to me, "Glasser, Helena's great, but why would you marry a girl who is exactly the same as you?"

Someone emerges from the shower. It is my turn. By the time I finish, the conversation has moved on, so I am never required to answer Mark's question until more than a decade later when I must stammer some explanation to my wide-eyed six-year-old daughter of how her parents' lives drained of purpose, and all I can offer is some incoherent nonsense about how people sometimes grow apart.

What might have I said to Mark? Helena and I were

in a fearsome hurry, blind and rushed as a sports car in pitch black night on a country road with a stoner at the wheel in a race against curfew. Courtship, marriage, and parenthood needed to be done with so we could move on to…what exactly? Helena seemed suitable to me, and I suppose I did to her, but we overlooked how some geometry problems have no solution: try to square a circle, go trisect an angle.

Our marriage careened through the night. Twists and turns loomed so fast from the darkness no one could predict the road. The soundtrack was about betrayal, lust, rage and flight, but even at top volume, we seemed not to have heard, but slept.

Helplessly Hoping
Crosby, Still, Nash, & Young

The paper in my father's lockbox may once have been white, but it had aged to a dull yellow, and the blue-black ink long ago had oxidized to rusty brown. The fountain pen script had great looping whorls on the Fs and Ls. Opened and refolded many times, the paper had grown so soft it parted at a crease. My father carefully patted the two fragile pieces smooth on the kitchen table, fitting them together as if they were intricately patterned wallpaper, a task at which he had a lifetime's experience. He would use no cellophane tape. "That crap dries up and curls," he explained. "Ruins everything."

The date at the page's bottom read *1930*, so he'd been eighteen when he wrote the poem about Anna, a girl in Staten Island. That was far from his haunts in the Bronx. With his two palms flat on the paper, he pivoted it toward me. At a kitchen table, my hands at my sides, I read my father's poetry.

It was goddam awful.

My parents had retired to Florida. I visited now and again. My mother, Muriel, took a daily stroll among the hydrangea-lined paths of their condo development. My father did not walk with my mother because he'd lost four toes to diabetes and so he was unsteady on his feet. While she was out, my father withdrew his lockbox from the bottom of a drawer bureau where it rested beneath several heavy sweaters schlepped from New York City, bulky knits my mother had stitched but no one would ever wear again. Like pharaohs in their burial chambers, in God's Waiting Room, Florida, retirees surround themselves with the props they'll require for eternity.

The lockbox also held a forged steel belt buckle, a brass corporate paper impression stamp left from the small business he had run, gold cufflinks, yellowed Kodak photos of me, my sister and brother— stuff that had no place in a bank safe deposit box. Dad just wanted the stuff nearby.

I am now 60. In my basement two black steamer trunks are labeled, "Destroy Without Opening." If you have not yet squirreled away such stuff, trust me, you will. And, trust me on this, too, should your house catch fire and fill with smoke, despite all good sense, you will rot your lungs and risk your life to rescue those trunks.

The poem was a hymn to Anna, a girl with merry green eyes and flashing yellow hair, how she walked, the music of her voice, her laugh, her smile, and the precise angle at which she held her chin. It described a narrative of sorts, but it was more metaphor than event; my father was the knight, Anna the damsel. The evil king may have been her father. Dad must have read a lot of stirring Kipling; his poem was a series of rhyming couplets, each couplet its own stanza, each stanza followed by a single, underlined word, *Excelsior!* At the final line, the word was underlined twice.

I was 36, exactly half my father's age as we sat across from each other in that sunny efficiency kitchen; exactly double his age when he wrote the poem. I just realized that strange concurrence of numbers while I write this; the stars were aligned on multiples of eighteen, the Jewish number that means *Life*.

By then I knew my name would never appear on the short list for the Nobel Prize for Literature. I had achieved some small distinction with a first book and a handful of writing awards (a very small handful, to be sure), the foundations of an academic career. My mother kept my book in a translucent envelope that also held my elementary school report cards until I asked her to place the book prominently in the living room. "Let your neighbors see it," I told her, and when she explained, "I am saving it for you," I had to point out that I was not likely to run out of copies any time soon. She laughed without appreciating my irony at nonexistent sales, but after that, my first book stood spine out on a shelf beside a green glass vase they'd bought in Florence, Italy, a few neighbors remarked on it, and one or two asked for copies, which I dutifully supplied, free.

But here was my father asking me about poetry. He was asking me as a writer, not his son. It was a literary conversation; my opinion mattered.

What did I think?

When I'd been a college student, Dad belittled me for planning to become anything so ordinary as a high school English teacher—never mind that the job would keep me out of Vietnam's jungles. Ten years of inner-city kids trapped by grim lives broke my heart before I left teaching to become a student again. I attended graduate school to pursue a dream too long deferred.

Dad's contempt had been ferocious.

My idiocy not only meant I was absconding from New York City to godforsaken Arizona with his youngest grandchild and my wife, it meant I was selling a house and abandoning a perfectly secure job to become a dreamer, a goddam dreamer, maybe becoming a total fucking idiot. *Will you be moving to Paris any time soon?*

For several months before we set out for Tucson, talk with my parents echoed my earliest teens, back to a time when over dinner one night I'd expressed a vague desire to become an intellectual. I might have been fifteen. Kennedy was in the White House collecting a Cabinet of eggheads. After some general laughter that I even knew such a word, Dad became red in the face telling me how stupid I was. But the word *intellectual* was new to me: I liked the feel of it. I would smoke a pipe and dwell in an unsullied realm of thought. I was a math whiz, but some English teacher had already begun luring me to the Dark Side by having me read Millay, and, like her, I understood *Euclid alone has looked on Beauty bare*. Somehow, pursuing the life of the mind would propel me into the future.

At every opportunity through high school and college, my father applied ridicule to me like a strap. He could say *intellectual* in a way that made it sound as if it was something that had fallen from the rear of a barnyard animal. And his sneering scorn amused his wife, my mother. No provocation was needed for me to become dinner table sport. So years later, when at 30 I announced I was leaving for Tucson, Arizona to write, his first response was his familiar, theatrical slap to his forehead and to say, "There goes the *intellekshu-all!*"

Well, what boy and his father have an easy time of it?

By the time we sat in his Florida kitchen, his blood had cooled and his tongue softened. Age spots flowered on his forehead and face, his eyes had grown shallow and rheumy, his arms once taut with muscle hung with loose flesh. He suffered the endless indignities of growing old without complaint, the doctors sawing away at him, removing parts made moribund by diabetes as if he were a rotting tree. If they took his legs, he joked, we could count the rings to discover exactly how old he really was.

Now he offered up his treasure to me, this poem about this Anna.

What did I think?

David Glasser, my father, was born three days before HMS Titanic sank. I don't know when his father was born, but other than being alive at the time of the Astors and Guggenheims, Louis Glasser had no connection to the Gilded Age. A corporal in the army of the Emperor Franz Joseph, Louis showed good sense, went AWOL, and fled.

I am the youngest of three children, and all of us, including our parents, called my father's father Little Louis. Little Louis was dead before I was six, so all I recall is a frail old man with Juicy Fruit gum and shiny pennies in his pockets. I was once in the dark hovel where he lived in Coney Island with a woman my mother and father barely acknowledged; I don't believe she was ever invited to our apartment in Brooklyn. Dad was there to drop off table money, and in that marginal neighborhood was unwilling to leave me to wait in the car. I was an adult before I realized the woman who put the folded bills between her loose breasts under a housecoat might have been more than a nurse. I recall Little Louis at our place on one occasion being embarrassingly incontinent, but like all of us, he must have known a time when he expected to live forever. Bold enough to leave the Old World, in the New he'd made a living delivering seltzer, a job that required him to bend double beneath several wooden cases loaded with thick, pressurized bottles before toting them up flights of tenement stairs. He carried three or four cases at each trip, twelve bottles to the case, and the weight of the blue, yellow and clear glass siphons must have been crushing. Elevators were rare; the narrow, dark stairs would have been steep and uneven. In America, what horses, mules or trucks pulled through the streets, men toted up stairs: milk, ice, eggs, freshly slaughtered meat—even seltzer.

Seltzer, should you need to know, is carbonated water, an ingredient not only necessary for whiskey and soda, but for an egg-cream, a staple of New York City culture. Calling an *egg-cream* an *egg-cream soda* is a little like being in Philadelphia and asking for a *cheesesteak sandwich*. You are liable to get what you want, but the locals will cover smirks at the rube who does not know his *tuchas* from a hole in the ground. Order an egg-cream soda made with sparkling water, milk, and chocolate sauce, and expect a side order of condescension. Sparkling water? Please. *Sparkling water* is the stuff Dick Powell or Fred Astaire squirt into highball tumblers before a tuxedoed tap-dance through Times Square. No, an honest egg-cream jumps a trolley from downtown, is made with seltzer, for cryin' out loud, and begins with a dollop of Fox's U-Bet syrup, not some abomination called *chocolate sauce*. Should anyone offer to put an egg in your egg-cream, get up, just *get up*, get up and leave.

One of Little Louis's two sons became a doctor. My father, David, was the other one.

A thousand family stories chronicle my father's physicality, and I have no reason to doubt any of them. When he passed, his children sorted through family photographs, and we were struck by the height of the stack of pictures we made of Dave posed like a champion boxer, his two fists over his head, smiling into the camera, photos taken decades apart: on the boardwalk in Brighton Beach; in Canada with two of his young children seated on his biceps; a retiree standing in the jungle near the Aztec pyramids of Mexico.

Do not misunderstand me; Dad was physical, but he seldom struck his sons except for a single slap across the can, and he never struck his daughter or wife. As our mother expressed it, as a young man, David had been "quick to his hands." She relished the tale of how when some goon in the row behind them chattered through most of a movie, after twice asking him to keep it down, my father stood up and socked him in the jaw hard enough that the guy vaulted backward over a row of seats. "He looked like Firpo clobbering Jack Dempsey," my mother added, doing her best imitation of a bob and weave, and when Dad shushed her, I had to look it up at the library where I discovered a plate of the painting by George Bellows. It impressed me, violence made art.

As a teenager who worked summers with him doing the labor of a housepainter, I had a claim to fellowship. We sat on the grass in some client's backyard splitting a ham and swiss hero sandwich when I asked if the story were true.

"More or less," he said. He drank coffee from a thermos. "I don't know that he flew back a row. That's your mother's imagination at work." The pride of a middle-aged man at his roguish youth was absent from his voice. When he realized what he'd confessed to his boy, he added, "Times were different. You knew what to expect. No guns; no knives. Men were regular. Don't be stupid." He tore at a section of soft dough and handed me a larger share of our lunch.

In his mid-50s, Dad asked me to teach him to play tennis. He had played handball most of his life. That archetypical Depression sport required only a callused palm, a black rubber ball, sneakers, and a wall. Tennis was for sissies. Not only did you play tennis at country clubs, but you had to wear white. What kind of poof wears white shorts?

I knew tennis because starting at ten for eight weeks every summer I had been sent to summer camp. My summers at camp were not about country air. Summer camp was no luxury my family decided to lavish on their youngest: my father's bankruptcy returned my mother to the workforce. My tennis education was a byproduct of Dad's business failure and the family's need for my daycare.

By the late '60s, Dad was slowing down. Handball was too tough, but here was tennis, a game that extended an ageing man's reach by three feet. What was more, tennis was all the rage; Arthur Ashe, a black amateur wearing a pastel shirt ended the Australian hegemony by beating Rod Laver in the 1968 US Open. My older brother and sister took up the game. Suddenly, jokes that ended with an effete, "Tennis anyone?" no longer seemed hilarious. Billie Jean King would legitimize and make lucrative a professional sport for women by moving from the baseline, charging net, and playing the power game. In 1973, she defeated a fading male player, Bobby Riggs. The time's they were indeed a-changin'.

But Dad and I did not care that we surfed a wave of a social revolution. All I knew was that late one August day he'd persuaded me to drive him to the cracked concrete courts behind Mark Twain Junior High School on Neptune Avenue in Brooklyn. The late summer light was diminishing. I stared at him across what in a municipal park were laughingly called nets, maintenance-free strips of rigid cyclone fence strung between two poles.

These courts in a corner of south Brooklyn were obscure enough that only a few diehard players flailed away at each other in the thickening twilight. I'd shown up with a dozen dead tennis balls in a brown paper shopping bag, correctly predicting that in the course of the afternoon, Dad would swing away and launch several into orbit.

In my car, I'd suggested that with a racket he'd have to learn control and touch. He was skeptical. "Control" to his mind meant abandoning power, something he was loath to do. On the court, I'd given all the standard instruction: turn your shoulder to the net, step around a forehand, pivot on the ball of your foot, follow through and, maybe, just maybe, get some topspin. As a counselor at summer camp, I'd snaked my arm around the waists of any number of young girls, bent them forward and back to emphasize form, and with my hip had nudged their rears to show them how to shift their weight to their forward foot, but an arm around my father's waist, my chest to his back, guiding his body through a swing seemed the wrong tactic. So Dad stood square to the net, his weight poised unsteadily on his toes, wearing his black, high-top handball sneakers, and—I swear this is true—tossing his racket from his right hand to his left for a shot most people would attempt as a backhand. He was not about to give away his only asset, the ambidexterity he had from handball and the strength that comes from standing on a ladder while both arms handle paint brushes overhead. No backhand for him, thank you very much. Dad made the game his own.

A few people smiled at the father and son enjoying a day together. I was just past the age of feeling humiliated simply by being seen with him, and I did not mind being in a public situation where I was clearly his superior. I think now he truly believed that after a few hours, he'd be able to win, or at least, "Give you a run for your money."

That was not going to happen, but, truth, he was having a hell of a good time. He was getting a workout, the mutually agreed upon illusory premise with which I had agreed to teach him the game. We were there for the exercise, and after my rocky adolescence a little male bonding was in order.

But from my point of view, the afternoon was not all it could be. I had not broken a sweat, a fact that should have put his delusions that we were there for a workout to rest, but far worse was that I grew impatient with his chasing down the ball after every errant shot. I could not get any rhythm going. I waved to him to join me at net. I explained we had pissed off our neighbors enough that they had moved from an adjacent court to one at the far end of the enclosure. "They put three balls in the can for a reason," I said. "A player gets two chances on the serve for a reason. No one steals tennis balls. They have numbers printed on them so people can sort them out."

"You can't trust these wisenheimers," he said, waving at the entire universe. He noted for the first time the numeral imprinted in the tennis ball fuzz.

"Tennis is different," I said. "People even make line calls against themselves."

I was a hotdog-23, but at summer camp I had learned to appreciate the sense of nobility that came with making a close call against myself—and if that meant that my opponent was inclined to make the next close call in my favor, well, that was tennis.

"That would never work at handball," he told me. "The game is cutthroat."

He was right. The handball park where for decades my father had played Sunday mornings was known for gambling. My father liked thoroughbred racing, so he was no stranger to wagering, but he played handball for the sake of playing. He was a fixture at the Avenue P Park, trusted enough that he often held the money of active players. If he were in a doubles match, though he did not wager, it was understood and accepted that Dave would play his best. These were men who could lose ten straight points, take a water break while a friend laid money at longer odds, and then come back to reel off fifteen consecutive shoe-string rifle-shot services. Hustling was not limited to Brooklyn poolrooms. Hundreds could be laid on a single handball game. Guys named Sandler and Hershkowitz played at Avenue P, and between the two of them from the 1950's to the 1970's they shared more than twenty AAU championships. At that time and in that place, handball was far more than a workout.

Dad and I returned to our respective tennis baselines. I patted a few shots to him. His natural swing, besides being overpowering, was actually not all that bad. He was an athlete, a physical guy, no intellectual. Yes, his elbow was too stiff and his arm too fully extended, but he did turn at the waist. He swung like a weathervane with a wooden racket. But after the better part of an hour of my serving up ground strokes slow and fat as flying grapefruits, he grew impatient. Dad wanted to play. "For points. Give me your best game," he said.

I explained the scoring.

"What's this crap?" he said. "Fifteen for one point? Why can't we just do like ping-pong. The first person to get to twenty-one wins," he said, waved his hand dismissively and started to walk away, the matter settled.

"If we ever get into a doubles game and you say that," I called after him, "they will think you are an idiot." He turned and smiled, revealing his not-so-secret agenda, which was to get good enough that I'd adopt him as a doubles partner. He needed a sport to take him into old age, and here was a game all three of his children played.

Well, I could live with that, I thought.

He conceded the scoring. I told him he could serve first, indicated he should move to his left, explained the service box, and said, "Serve 'til you get one in."

He hit the ball underhand. It missed the box by a mile. His next half dozen tries either smacked into the net or fell short of the net altogether. Irritated, he tried overhand and sidearm. The balls either struck the fence behind me or sailed so far over my head they landed outside the tennis enclosure.

I grew bored. When an underhand serve finally landed in the box and bounced waist high, as he'd requested, I gave him my best game. I ripped a backhand crosscourt with full pace and topspin. It skidded off the concrete near his feet, bouncing no higher than his shin. He was astonished, standing so flat-footed that he did not even swing.

I waved him to the net again. "You can't serve underhand."

"Why not?"

"That's how girls serve," I said, desperate for an explanation. "It's too easy."

"Aaach. All right already. Show me how to serve."

I talked about a consistent toss, swinging through overhead at the top of an arc, and then, inspired, I said, "Just hang the racket behind your ear and throw a football."

"Throw a football?"

"Yeah. Serving in tennis is the same motion as throwing a football."

"I can do that."

"Just stay balanced. Keep your front foot pointed at the net post."

"Same as football?"

"Same as football."

Dad came of age in the 1920s and '30s on Webster Avenue near the Grand Concourse in the Bronx. He swam in the Hudson, a clear river. A high school kid, he'd mixed mostly with his Irish friends, and as a middle-aged man, he liked telling us about them. He did this so frequently that my brother, sister and I could finish his stories for him, which we did, mercilessly. The tales had mythic status at our family table, these stories of McPartland, Kennelly, and Lennon, boys ever-ready to mix it up with their common enemies, boys who'd grown into tired, sad-eyed men together. In their day, my father claimed that before an Irish wedding they agreed to meet at the door once the fight started, an event that never failed to materialize. On St. Patrick's Day, my mother boiled corned beef and cabbage.

A framed photo of Dave with a fat lip and two black eyes hangs on my living room wall to this day. He stands on a grassy field, and he wears a jersey with pants that extend to his shin. He wears cleats. The photo is mounted on heavy cardboard, creased at one corner. Dave played football for DeWitt Clinton High School, and the photo, I believe, was taken after a game.

So never mind having Irish friends at a time when anti-Semitism was ordinary; my father played football in an era when the famous Seven Granite Blocks of Fordham, a national collegiate football power located in the Bronx, had players with names like Lombardi, Jacunski, and Wojciechowicz. Football was played by Polack coal miners, Eye-talians, Micks, and Cossacks, not Yids. And my father must have been good, because the College of William and Mary in Virginia offered him an athletic scholarship.

For two years, at the same school that had educated Washington and Jefferson, my father played fullback on the freshman and then varsity squads, going both ways, offense and defense. Dad took pride pointing out to his children that that was how the game was played in those times. But in 1932, the Depression and his mother's death saw Little Louis pull David from Williamsburg back to Webster Avenue. Someone had to tend house.

Snatched from athletic glory at college, my father cooked, cleaned, shopped and pumped gasoline, another job that required muscle. Pumps were manual. At a corner gas station, my father with two hands and his back turned a stubborn crank for Standard Oil of New Jersey, Mr. Rockefeller's oil monopoly that became ESSO, and then Exxon.

In my father's world, men fought with their hands to impress their girls; gasoline was pumped by hand; every football player was expected to run, catch, throw, block, kick, and tackle. They were regular guys.

So the 72-year-old man in God's Waiting Room who wanted to know what I really thought of his poem had been a fearless, physical young man, an athlete as versatile as Jim Thorpe. The poem I'd never seen seemed not to fit what I knew. "Did you write this in college?" I asked the frail man who fixed his glasses and silently reread his work. His lips moved as he read.

"In summer. Just after high school," he told me.

"Just before you went to college," I said.

He withdrew the forged belt buckle from the lockbox and showed me how the leather would have looped through a metal clasp. The buckle read *William and Mary*. For a laugh, he placed his gray and green freshman beanie on his bald head. His years as a painting contractor, he'd run the W&M Painting Company—the brass seal all that remained of his entrepreneurial venture, its bankruptcy, and the years my mother groused about riding in a vehicle that left the stink of turpentine lingering in her hair and on her children. I'm the youngest of three, I am the artist—my middle name is William.

I knew little of his two years in college. There was the tale of a loss to Navy in a driving rain. The field was soup, the turf soft and receptive, but at that game on a diving tackle his front teeth were permanently kicked backward; I also knew that he sold three-cent slices of dessert in the dining commons as part of his scholarship, plaintively calling out "Pi-aye! Pie for sale!" I also knew he had a roommate from Marblehead, Massachusetts, a man who claimed ancestry from the Pilgrims.

And that was all I knew.

"What did you major in?" I asked.

"English," he said, as if it were obvious. I'd never seen him read anything more complicated than *The Reader's Digest*. Maybe a man whose days were spent hauling and climbing ladders with the handles of five-gallon pots of paint in each hand was not eager to return home and engage his mind with Dickens or Tolstoy. Maybe with ridicule he'd hoped to spare me that life.

Dad carefully folded the beanie and ran his rough hand over his bald head. I considered what I should have always known.

Excelsior.

Dad asked, "What do you think of my poem? Really?"

I could have ripped the ball crosscourt past his ankles, left him flat-footed swinging at air. I could have done that, but I said, "It's not all that bad."

Not then, not even soon after, but only recently I forgave myself that lie.

Chalk

The Times They Are A-Changin'
Bob Dylan

When I first walked into Room 206 of Bay Ridge High School in Brooklyn, New York, in September 1969, I had with me two visible symbols of authority—a necktie and a fancy red loose-leaf binder that held five cardboard seating charts.

Both constricted my throat.

That first day as a teacher, I knew with absolute certainty what my sophomores from Puerto Rico, Haiti, the Dominican Republic, Colombia, Chile, Greece, Vietnam, Cambodia, Hong Kong, and Taiwan needed. I knew precisely what my juniors from the parishes of Louisiana and the black counties of Tennessee, South Carolina, and Georgia required. I knew without a doubt what was vital to my freshmen born in Brownsville, Crown Heights, and Sunset Park.

Relevance.

It was still the '60s. America was painfully aware that it was losing the trust of its youth. Since vast populations of young people on the other side of what was called the Generation Gap questioned authority, official educational policy was to demonstrate to young people how the daily reality that they knew was really and truly just the same as the reality of the people in charge. The apologists of Moloch, those spin-masters and public relation flacks of business and government, could sleep soundly assured that teachers as idealistic and naïve as I were indoctrinating youth with messages of relevance.

I planned to teach poetry by playing recordings by Bob Dylan and Paul Simon. I would teach writing, but I would respect the peculiar grammar of what we then called "ghetto English." My class discussions would be "rap sessions." Yes, the times, they were a-changin'.

Because of its ethnic makeup and impoverished reading scores, Bay Ridge High School was deemed a difficult-to-staff inner-city school, a category that kept me out of the jungles of Southeast Asia as I performed a public service equivalent to working in a defense plant.

It was a hell of a deal; you could not beat it with a stick. I delayed my irresistible assault on literary fame, evaded the draft, worked as a revolutionary, and collected a salary from the very Establishment I was at 21 dedicated to overthrow. I'd be boring through the rotting infrastructure of a dying culture from within. I'd bring the war back home. I'd teach as a subversive activity. A Bolshevik before the blackboard, my cause was not communism, but I would be the harbinger of the dawning of the Age of Aquarius. Let the sun shine in.

Delay of my own ambitions was to become a running theme of my life. Teaching high school kids was strictly a temporary accommodation, one that would last a mere temporary decade.

Not so incidentally, when I walked into that classroom, I discovered that every one of my students was a girl. The people at orientation a week earlier assumed I knew the nature of the school to which the Board of Education had assigned me.

I did not.

Bay Ridge High School was an anachronism. Two generations earlier, white immigrants—Irish, Scandinavian, Italian—required public schools exclusively for their daughters. Several such schools were in New York City, each paired with an entrance-examination boys' school, but shrinking enrollments, shifting demographics, and political pressures were doing their work. The girls in my classrooms did not enroll at Bay Ridge because they required a certain delicate education before marriage; rather, my students were sent to Bay Ridge by parents fearful for their daughters' safety in neighborhood schools. As long as we had a seat, no girl from Brooklyn could be turned away. They traveled considerable distances by public transportation, fleeing violence. Most were happy to be admitted.

One week after first report cards, we scheduled parent/teacher conferences. Don't visualize the suburban version of this event: at Bay Ridge High School, long lines of anxious parents waiting for a hurried, whispered conversation with a teacher did not exist. Though 170 students were enrolled in my five classes, if I met with three parents in the two-and-a-half hours set aside for conferences, I was considered to have had a busy evening. A few of my colleagues griped about parents who didn't give a damn, but most of us knew that many people didn't show up simply because they were worn out after a day's labor, they were often single mothers with large families who could not afford a babysitter, and they had not had a great deal of positive experience with city agencies of any kind. The Welfare Department, the Unemployment Bureau, and the Board of Education were perceived as tentacles of the same octopus—the City.

Despite the promised low attendance, these interviews caused me considerable anxiety. It was difficult enough to get my students to take me seriously, though the tie did help. They guessed I was an old man of 25, and I did not correct them. But how could I hope to fool parents? They would see that I was no more than a 21-year-old kid learning to teach. My department Chair gave me one piece of advice. "Keep them talking," Harold said, "and they'll think you are brilliant. Ask about their ambitions for their little charmer."

The black woman who waddled into my classroom toward the end of that night must have weighed 250 pounds. She was my one and only visitor. Her green hat looked like a plate of mashed beans, and it was pinned to the side of her head. Despite the superheated air of the school, she wore her gray cloth coat because the school supplied no place where she could hang it. Her shapeless shoes might have been black cardboard boxes. Her legs were sheathed by some sort of coarse, white nylon hose rolled below her knee.

I looked up and smiled encouragingly.

She scowled.

When she sat heavily on the chair to the left of my

desk, she scarcely fit on it. Her breath whistled through her nose, and she took a moment to catch her breath before she explained to me that she had had no patience to wait for the elevator and so had climbed to the top floor to start with the teachers there. She had then walked to the fourth floor, then the third, and now at last she was on the second floor. I was Mr. Glasser, right? The English teacher? She checked the white index card in her hands. Rivulets of perspiration flowed down both sides of her round face behind her ears and into her collar.

She settled back on the tiny chair. Had I known any of her other daughters? She had sent four to the school, and this one, this last girl, was her problem child.

I said I was new to the school, and, when her deep-set eyes held mine, she saw me for the first time. She did not have to say anything for me to learn what she thought. We both knew that when her oldest had attended this high school, I'd been a high school student myself.

Though she had summed me up with a glance, she was humble and respectful, so much so that it made conversation awkward. I knew from her daughter that this woman raised her children alone, that her four children had three fathers, and that she worked for a commercial cleaning company. By night, she scrubbed the tile floors and toilets in lavatories in Manhattan office buildings. I also knew that none of her children had gone to college and that the daughter in my class, a decent enough kid, was feeling terrific pressure to do so. This was a time when New York City still operated its extensive college system free of charge for city residents; however, in my broadly based experience and finely honed professional judgment of two months, I had decided that her daughter, a junior, lacked the stuff to make it—even to a community college. I'd been talking up typing and stenography.

I would share no such wisdom with her mother, however. The woman before me listened intently as I read out her daughter's grades, and she nodded when I said that I was sure that her child could do better if she applied herself. I asked about television. I asked about homework. I asked whether her daughter had a good, quiet place to study in the evening.

Appreciate how fraudulent this conversation was. I knew it, and she knew it. It was late fall in 1969, and what her daughter's world was about was dance clubs, the platform shoes my students called CFMs, sex, pregnancy, and pills—mostly reds, that is, downers. CFMs? Yvonne, a student, taught me the abbreviation; the heels on their shoes forced a stance on a girl, ass out, boobs forward, calves taut, a stance that said, "Come Fuck Me." This woman's apartment was at the top of a three-story walkup in a neighborhood where sirens, babies, and battered wives wailed all night. Parental supervision? A quiet place to study? Making sure her daughter did not watch too much television? The woman before me started her shift at 10:00 every evening. She would leave this conference with me and ride a subway directly to work. She'd arranged to arrive late this night, though she would be docked an hour's pay. When she returned home, after sunrise, her daughter would be awakening. Perhaps mother and daughter would pass at the door. If by the time her daughter was 18 she had not become a junkie, a mother, a whore, or any combination of those three, the woman before me could be proud of the job she'd done.

Our conversation was finished, but she did not rise to her feet. I seized on my chairman's advice. "What are your plans for your daughter?" I asked.

The glaze of fatigue and defeat evaporated from her eyes. She leaned toward me and spoke slowly. "I want her to have your job," she said.

Unsure that I had heard her properly, I asked again.

"Your job," she repeated, leaning toward me. "You wear nice clothes. You don't sweat. You don't bend, and you don't stoop. Am I right?"

I said that she was.

Her lips pursed, she sat back, and she nodded an "Amen" as she would on Sunday mornings when the minister recited from the Book. "That's what I want for my girl," she said.

I smiled and said that her daughter would have a long way to go.

She sidled further forward on the tiny chair, so close now that I could feel her breath when she spoke, but I could not move back.

"That's what I wanted to talk to you about," she whispered. "To get your job, you have to know Shakespeare, am I right? The hard stuff. Am I right?"

I nodded.

She patted my hand. "So what I wants to know is just why the school keeps sending my daughter home with crap." I believe I was still smiling, but it was an effort. "She knows 'bout landlords. She knows 'bout gangs and whatnot. She don't need to be reading 'bout such trash. She needs to know what she *don't* know. If my girl is going to get your job, you need to give her everything. Not some watered down version for black folk. Same as you. Same as you. Get her to where you are, so she can pass you by. You see what I'm saying?"

So much for relevance.

She patted the back of my wrist before she pulled herself to her feet. "We understand each other," she said, nodded, and left.

I wish I could tell you that her daughter went on to become a neurosurgeon, but I can't. For all I know, she did, but I have no idea what became of her. Names vanish, faces fade; theories come, theories go. Tides move in, and tides move out. The years pass, and the rhetoric of education sprouts, blooms, wilts, and washes away. Some new edu-biz bright-light is always eager to blaze a new path, reposition the walls in classrooms, revamp accreditation standards, maybe sell a few new textbooks, publish an article or two, make a career.

Real teachers remember only one thing. When the classroom door is closed, students have to know who you are, and you have to be prepared to deliver everything you know. Not half. Not some. All of it.

Like love.

Layla
Derek and the Dominoes

It was a trite scene from a trite movie. While I lurked in murky shadows beneath the balcony, with absolute concentration a 16-year-old woman played the piano below stage left. You'd get Rachmaninoff or Grieg in the movie, but this was real life, and so the kid was feeling her way through the piano cadenza of "Layla," the Eric Clapton song newly on the radio. The solid chords echoed in the vast, empty hall. She was terrific. She played it twice, the second time injecting the piece with fresh, original passion.

When I stepped into the light and slowly clapped my hands, the sound echoed in the large hall as her head spun toward the applause. Her smooth, shoulder length brown hair flared out, exposing like a flash of light in the dim hall her round face. The piano fell shut, and she did what any smart high school kid in the wrong place at the wrong time does when a teacher shows up: she beat it.

All she left behind were a tiny hasp and hinge, a broken lock, three tiny brass screws that had been anchored in the piano's black wood, and the shattered Bic pen she'd used to pry them loose. My fingertips traced the raw wood of the splintered screw holes. They felt like rough wounds.

Twenty-three, married eighteen months, I was in my third year of teaching English, a job that not only set me before five classes of girls each day, but included forty minutes of building patrol. In a dim corridor behind the rear entrance to our Auditorium, a 500-seat balconied theater with oiled mahogany wall panels, stained glass windows, and two-story high blackout curtains, I loosened wads of notebook paper crumpled in fire door locks, and I flicked those balls of paper out to the street, allowing the doors to slide firmly, irrevocably shut on half-day truants and a few girls who'd ducked out for a quick smoke. This assignment was not as good as free time, but it beat Cafeteria Duty cold, and afterwards, I could hang out on the stage steps and grade a few papers.

Years later, Yolanda told me she had never had a music lesson, but taught herself on an upright at a YWCA. "But you'd be more impressed to see me dance," she said and she touched my wrist. "Salsa," she said, "Hot sauce." We must have by then been old friends; it was not the kind of touch you gave your high school English teacher.

But I never saw her dance, not even as a guest at her wedding. Her brocade and beaded gown was too heavy for anything more than a waltz or foxtrot. For this Puerto Rican bride trailing a lace mantilla, those Anglo excuses for movement could not even bring her to her feet.

And the last time I saw Yolanda, I asked if she thought I might ever see her dance salsa. She thought seriously about what had been a long-standing joke between us before she slowly said, "No." To dance like that in front of her former teacher—it would embarrass her.

That humid July night, we were not covered by as much as a sheet. Her bare shoulder nestling against my damp chest, my semen seeping from her, our hips slippery where they touched, without irony she determined to hold that final intimacy from me. A mystery in reserve made certain I understood that the gift I had received, a gift granted when I had never needed anything more, the gift that saved me, was a gift bestowed for complicated reasons.

Soon after I startled Yolanda at the piano, she landed in one of my classes. She devoured ideas ferociously. Once in a great while, you get a student like that. Ask any teacher. It's always breathtaking.

By a conspiracy of silence we established a polite fiction that I had never witnessed an act of vandalism, and so I was accorded a significant measure of trust. One afternoon, after forty minutes of inducting bored acolytes into the mysteries of the paragraph, I found Yoli waiting for me beside my desk. There was a personal problem. Did I have time? We made some appointment, but before she turned to go, I asked the nature of the problem. Frail as bird wings, her narrow shoulders moved uncertainly beneath her aquamarine blouse. It was a small matter. She needed to decide exactly who she was and who she would be; could I help with that?

My incoming class had some sort of set-up assignment scrawled on the chalkboard—the "Do Now"—so I stepped into the emptying hallway with Yolanda and asked for more details.

At her meetings of the Puerto Rican Liberation Party, several of the women believed Yolanda wasn't Puerto Rican enough. Mostly it was her complexion. That had forever pissed off both her darker sisters, too. "I'm a pale PR with a stick up my ass," she said and shrugged.

With books crushed to her chest, her straight brown hair pulled tight to a ponytail, her skin what the good folks at Crayola then called Flesh, her face round, her enormous eyes magnified by the faintly pink glasses she wore on her almost straight, slightly bulbous nose, Yolanda looked like a Jewish Barnard student.

I could not understand her problem. I called into the classroom that my students should exchange papers and read each others' responses, a dodge I could justify as peer editing. Yolanda sighed. The Party was a Marxist-Leninist-Maoist activist cell dedicated to the liberation of Puerto Rico, a goal to which Yolanda totally subscribed. Politics and *Yanqui* capitalism had destroyed her father, a political functionary unemployed and unemployable ever since an election went badly in Ponce. Other men waited and worked to be re-elected; her father found solace in rum. Her family had journeyed to Nueva York because an uncle took pity. Papi managed the uncle's hardware store, a job her father found humiliating. Sometimes the Party met at the church, sometimes other places. I must have seen that she often wore a red beret, did I think that was some sort of stupid fashion statement? They admired Fidel, they adored Che. Yolanda had come to the Party through her older brother, Paco, who no longer lived at home with Papi and Mammi and Yolanda's two sisters. There was no telling where or when Paco might reappear. He was really only a half-brother, anyway, a dark brother, features like a black man, probably why willingly last summer Paco volunteered to burn cane in Cuba, not only to further the cause of Socialism, but to rediscover his slave roots.

The Party cell to which Yolanda belonged met for monthly self-criticism sessions, and this past weekend when Yolanda could think of nothing to say, some *puta* who had been the cell leader's girlfriend ragged for half an hour about Yolanda's need to be more Puerto Rican. Being so pale and all, Yolanda was not unawake to this possibility, but since the cell leader had been, you know, suggesting things to her, things about this and that, suggestions she did not at all mind hearing, Yolanda wondered if maybe his ex old lady was using the criticism session less to make pure the cell's revolutionary fervor and more to vent her personal jealousy.

I wondered if she were putting me on. How could her complexion annoy her sisters? I stuck my head into the half-open door of my class and instructed them to read further in their book—an exercise called directed study. "From where?" some kid asked, and I recall saying "From wherever you are," before I returned my attention to Yolanda.

So, in a hallway, while I should have been attending to the education of thirty or so other kids, one uppity pale PR taught me about racism within a Puerto Rican family. With a touch of impatience, Yolanda explained the well-known fact that notions of beauty were culturally derived, and that a subject people, such as the people of Puerto Rico, would have a concept of beauty forced upon them that would make them despise themselves. But a dedicated people could discover their own beauty, would come to regard themselves as strong, and so in this way throw off the yoke of the imperialist oppressor. "Like 'Black is Beautiful,'" I said, and she looked sideways at me. "Yeah, like that, but for the people of Puerto Rican, it is much more complicated." There was slave African blood and Castilian conquistador blood and mysterious *Indio* blood and even despised *Yanqui* blood, the consequence of rape. As a member of the ruling oppressor class, I could not hope to understand such things, though she appreciated my efforts.

Her sisters were pale, too, though Magalla's hair was coarse, and Enid's perfect Anglo features were shaped in skin dark as coffee. They called Enid "the Arab." No one knew what to make of Magalla, she was so smart she was spooky. Yolanda suspected Magalla could read books in her sleep. Nevertheless, their father clearly favored Yolanda; *la bonita*, the pretty one. Now, Yolanda understood the political necessity for redefining beauty in revolutionary terms, but in a mirror what she saw persisted in looking good to her. All the meetings in the world could never change that opinion. Her face made her heart reactionary. What she wanted to know from me, her gringo English teacher whose soul was maybe not totally corrupt, was whether she was smart enough and white enough to get by in the world as a white person. It would betray a principle, but no other choice was available to her. What was it like to be a white person? Was it as boring as it seemed?

You can get questions like these from sincere 16-year-olds. Anyone who has been a high school teacher knows what I am talking about. Kids require answers. When it comes to themselves, they are humorless.

I recited pieties about how identity was a personal matter, and I mouthed some drivel about how much I appreciated her trust.

The students beyond the oak door jumped around like dolphins in a tank, but I had forgotten them, for my imagination was aflame with the romantic possibilities of Yolanda's life. Despite the evidence I saw daily at my job, a part of me still wanted to believe that poverty germinated wonderful, beautiful, hopeless causes that could lift a person above the petty concerns of self, causes for which words like "dedication," "sacrifice," and "liberation" could be uttered without blush. Her world was dark, dangerous, dirty and violent, and I was young, stupid, bored, and privileged enough to think that grand.

When the bell rang, we still chatted in the hallway. In this way, thirty or so students were deprived of forty minutes of education because their English teacher could not abandon one pale PR in the hall.

I suppose worse things have happened.

Over the years, I would see Yolanda and with diminishing seriousness ask how went the revolution, and she would with equally diminishing seriousness answer about changes in the Party line. Initially over coffee and in later years over beer, in strictly theoretical ways we discussed the illusion of private property, the necessity for violence to effect change, and whether pigs had wings. I studied television coverage of this rally or that, hoping to discover her face in the background, convinced her appearance on TV would magically validate my vicarious connection to issues of justice and freedom, so much more meaningful than the quibbles of my petty life, casualty insurance, retirement fund contributions, and exploring better commuter routes to Brooklyn from the new condo my wife and I had purchased in northern New Jersey.

I confronted my tolerance for real risk about two years after Yolanda graduated from high school. She'd made Harvard; the only person surprised by this was she. Near Christmas, she'd come down from Cambridge and found time to meet me for an hour or two in Greenwich Village. Over salads and bitter dark beer, Yolanda outlined for me the latest turns in her life—her family, *la revolucion*, and her new fiancée, an Hispanic medical school student. I dropped her off at some nondescript building on East 23rd Street. As my car slowed, she told me to wave and smile to the two men in an illegally parked black car across the street. They wore ties and gray fedoras and pointed a Leica with a long lens at us. I asked who they were. "FBI. CIA. Some Republicans. Who knows? They are always here," she said, "This is Party headquarters." She stepped lightly onto the sidewalk.

I'd done nothing more subversive than any taxi driver in New York, but for days I suffered night sweats. I'd be reading my censored mail in a Leavenworth cellblock. Sleepless, I watched news reports, convinced any bank robbery or airport explosion would bring the authorities to my door, curious to know what I knew of the young woman in the red beret and calf high boots who had stepped so nimbly from my Dodge. I prepared alibis. I would explain I was a friend to the family, a former teacher who offered counsel when it was wanted, and this answer, I realized in a moment of dizzying panic, might implicate me as the Trotsky of the Popular Front for the Liberation of Puerto Rico unless I explained precisely how this relationship came about.

It was an innocent tale. The August after Yolanda received her high school diploma, before she departed for Cambridge, she arrived at my Sheepshead Bay apartment door with both her sisters in tow. My wife and I would not migrate to New Jersey for two years more; Arizona was not even a fantasy. The three girls had been headed for Manhattan Beach, so when Magalla had been overcome by summer heat, the subway, and menstrual cramps, Yolanda steered them to our air-conditioned apartment after finding the address in a telephone book. Yolanda was eighteen, Magalla was fifteen, and Enid was barely pubescent, an intense little girl with great black eyes who stepped into the white teacher's air-conditioned place and sat motionless on a Queen Anne chair, sipping water, silent, afraid to move for fear she might break something fragile and expensive. The Arab. My wife administered aspirin and water and rest. After an hour or so, the sisters went on their way.

My telephone went untapped. Life churned on, making clearer with each day that my panic was simply another manifestation of narcissism, this need to believe myself to be fated to be at the center of great events.

While Yoli grappled with matters of justice, my wife and I debated decorator-suggested swatches for upholstery. Yoli imagined birthing a new world order; we planned our first child. Yoli wrestled with her race and heritage; I diversified our growing portfolio.

By the time Yolanda was a junior at Harvard, her sister Enid was a student at the high school. To my eye, Enid was prettier, but as a member of the ruling class it was likely my standards of beauty were perverted by my attraction to the exotic. Her eyes were perfectly black, and her lashes were long and fine.

But where Yolanda had been a ferocious student, Enid at fourteen was a listless junkie.

At the school, she avoided me. She had already suffered any number of teachers who on first meeting her would brighten at the memory of her two gifted older sisters and directly or indirectly communicate their impossible expectations for Enid. It must have been awful for her. Magalla, who was two years older than Enid, was truly the smart one and attended a special high school, and Enid's oldest sister, Yolanda, had gifts that had taken her to Cambridge. Back in Bushwick, only heroin's warm embrace enfolded Enid in unqualified love.

I sometimes saw the skinny guy who waited for Enid at the end of her school day, a mean-looking punk, short, restless, bouncing on the toes of his sneakers, the kind who thinks he has to be extra tough to compensate for lack of physical stature. To be free of truancy laws, two days beyond her sixteenth birthday, Enid officially dropped from high school. After she filed the paperwork, she found me to say goodbye. As dark and taciturn as ever, in her fifth month of pregnancy she was prettier than I'd ever seen her, though her dark eyes had gone shallow and hard as slate. Later, Yolanda told me that Enid's boyfriend turned her out to whore even while she carried the child.

Enid was absent from Yolanda's wedding.

Magalla, however, was present. During the five minutes she spent with us, after my wife conversationally asked how she had been, Magalla told her story to the kind people who had given her aspirin one brutal summer day. She sat knee to knee with me, gently holding both my hands in her own, her unswerving eyes focused on mine.

In May, just months before Yolanda's wedding and weeks before her own high school graduation, she had run off to Denver with her high school math teacher, an act whose timing lost her a full semester of school. She'd missed Regents Examinations; she'd missed finals. Such a mess! She would be graduating late, but nevertheless expected to attend Yale. Yolanda's experience at Harvard had demonstrated how much a Puerto Rican woman with ability could expect in scholarship money. Magalla predicted (and eventually obtained) room, board, tuition, books, and free transportation to and from New Haven. Her high school Math teacher, a sweet, simple man, abandoned his wife and two children for her, but after three weeks, she became bored with snow-capped mountains and so returned to Bushwick, a place she found far more engaging than Vail. She had no idea what had happened to him—a thing past, for Magalla, was past. Initially, the principal had thought it best that Magalla continue her education elsewhere, but after Magalla expressed her conviction that the special high school's diploma would enhance her admission chances to Yale, and after she expressed her sincere desire to put the whole matter behind her rather than explain to courts and press and whatnot the details of how a high school girl had been whisked off to Colorado by a 38-year-old Geometry teacher, the principal agreed it might be best to allow Mags to continue her studies. The whispers that followed her through the school's halls never came from fellow students, who knew nothing, but from a few female teachers. The men—and her voice tinkled with mirth—the men followed her only with their eyes.

And didn't Yoli look wonderful? It was good she would make this marriage. Perhaps she would abandon these stupid politics that preoccupied her life and carve out some comfort for herself. Ideals had ruined Paco—and now God alone knew where he was. Enid? She did not know of Enid's whereabouts, though she knew her young sister had given birth to a girl, up for adoption before they so much as allowed her to hold the shaking infant even once.

I saw even less of Yolanda after her wedding, naturally enough, and by then I was more than half through the decade I would spend as a high school teacher. I was troubled. The Vietnam War ended; once I was no longer in danger of being drafted, justifications for what I was doing were impossible to invent. When would I get on with my life? Why was I postponing? No matter what I was doing—teacher, husband, soon-to-be father—I had the eerie feeling I should be doing something else.

Left too long in confining cages, monkeys will compulsively, repeatedly masturbate. Too much of this drives them psychotic. They hurl shit through the bars. They soil their food, and, with fingernails, gouge wounds on their faces and arms, any sensation, even pain, preferred to lethargy.

I was one bored monkey.

I had an affair. As a sin, adultery is simple. It requires no talent, some capacity for self-deception, and modest daring. As it happens, these are the identical qualities necessary for admission to a graduate creative writing program.

I got in easy.

In Arizona a year, reading an eight-page hand-written letter, I learned Yolanda's marriage was failing, *La Revolucion* was dead, and after six years as an undergraduate, she quit Harvard a few credits shy of receiving her degree. I called; her telephone was disconnected. When I wrote back, my letter was forwarded to San Juan, but she had already moved from an address there and left no forwarding address this second time. After floating through the postal service for two months, my long, encouraging, newsy, happy letter returned to me, the envelope covered with yellow forwarding labels and a final, forbidding red postal stamp, "addressee unknown."

After a decade of intermittent conversation, Yolanda was vanished, lost in the Brownian movement of American lives.

Had she received my letter, she'd have read a fraud. Not that I had written anything to mislead her—I had believed every word. But during the months my letter wandered through the postal system, back in the desert, I was learning the cost of real risk—even quietly vulgar sin has consequences. While I pedaled my bicycle up and down the desert hills around Tucson, sang to my daughter strapped securely in the kid seat mounted over the rear wheel, and filled myself with assurance that I had come through something and arrived somewhere and that it was a good place to be, Helena was going mad.

She had forgiven me with her mind, and we had assumed her heart would follow, a logic majestic in its stupidity. Maybe if just once she had let loose and screamed, or just once thrown my sorry ass out the door, Helena would have purged herself of the acidic anger that lay dammed and swelling in her liver, curdling into self-hatred, but she had been raised to be a good girl, dutiful, restrained, and forgiving, and that, far more than my behavior, filled her with self-loathing. "I will not live my mother's life," she shouted and stormed out of a counseling session.

We divorced. Within weeks, Helena remarried.

I fled east for a one-month visit to my family with our daughter, Jessica, before I went off to my new life and new career in a new place. After that summer visit, I would be required to deliver our kid back to her mother. Driving through empty miles of interstate, I brooded on how my efforts at self-dramatization were worthless, inadequate, stupid, guilty, obtuse, inept, and had brought me only pain and ruin, a price to be extracted mostly from my partner sleeping in the passenger seat, my kid, Jessica.

The visit east went badly. There was no explaining to my parents the forces that had culminated in my failed marriage, nor could they accept that such a thing could happen without my direct, singular culpability. I had failed, and there could be no more to it. There was a vicious argument. Jessica will forever remember our being thrown out of my father's house, a late night drive, and our taking refuge at my sister's home.

So I had a week to kill before returning west. Looking up old friends, the crowd my wife and I had known, proved painful. At those gatherings, there was only one topic of conversation. I got a low-level charge of martyrdom by describing my ex's new husband, but the smidgen of sympathy made me feel cheap.

On a whim, from the telephone in my sister's bedroom, I called the last number I had that connected me to Yolanda—her mother's. I had not seen or heard from Yoli in nearly three years. *Mirabile dictu*, Yolanda herself answered the telephone. She was 27, divorced more than a year, recently back from the Island, living with her mother while she settled in. She had an office job in Manhattan, answering telephones and filing. It was nothing, but it was something. It was odd to hear from me, and she must have detected the note of desperation in my voice when I asked if we could get together, because she hesitated before she said, "Sure." We made arrangements. We would meet in Queens, after work.

In the crowd of commuters, I almost missed the woman who stepped from the elevated train platform. The girl I'd startled at the piano was round faced; this woman in clicking heels and narrow black dress was hollow-cheeked. Except at her wedding, I could not remember Yolanda with make-up other than lip-gloss and perhaps a touch of rouge; this New Yorker plucked her eyebrows, knew the ways of mascara, and had applied color and powder in an effort to lighten the shadows under her eyes. The college revolutionary who assumed the eventual triumph of her cause had laughed at the FBI; this woman's face was etched with fatigue and defeat. She was four years older than I had been the day I'd lurked in a balcony's shadow to listen to her find the chords of a rock song. More than a decade had passed, though the lyric had become painfully accurate:

What'll you do when you get lonely
And nobody's waiting by your side?
You've been running and hiding much too long.
You know it's just your foolish pride.

She hugged me lightly and led me away from my parked car. I could leave it on the street where I'd parked. This was not Bushwick. She and her mother lived in a safe Irish-Italian neighborhood. No one bothered her mother. Yoli knew a quiet bar nearby.

The place was cool and nearly empty, the kind with beer signs whose electric dots of colors crawl around the edge of a clock. The jukebox was overdosed on Frank Sinatra. We sat on red vinyl stools. Yoli ordered a Martini. It seemed the wrong drink for her, but, of course, given who she had become, it was nothing extraordinary. Her glasses were gone; she wore contacts. When she lighted a slender menthol cigarette, I hardly blinked.

So we caught up. When she met her husband, he had promised he would return to the Island and practice pediatrics in a free clinic, but as his residency had drawn to a close, a private practice in Boston had made him a lucrative offer. A doctor who spoke Spanish brought in many, many patients. There was money to be made. He and Yoli argued. He said he could do as much for their people by staying on the mainland, but Yolanda did not believe it. Feeling betrayed, she left school and returned to Puerto Rico alone, but there was no longer any revolution, she was unsure there ever had been, there was only politics. Justice? Nonsense. Everyone simply wanted a bigger piece. She'd followed Maggie's advice and became the mistress of a rich man, but she'd been sick with self-disgust. In that time, she came to understand her father, the drunk, and her sister, the junkie. She would never understand Maggie, who was finishing law school. Enid was probably dead. No one knew. Returned to Boston, Yolanda learned her husband had divorced her on grounds of desertion and taken up with another woman. He offered Yolanda some money, not a lot, but she took it. She bought some clothes. She paid some debts. A chapter of her life closed. She believed that could happen. She was grateful.

She looked at photos of my daughter, whom she had seen only once as an infant in my arms. Her eyes softened—here was something she hoped would someday happen with her. As I told her about the divorce, her fingers rested lightly on the back of my hand. It was not a seductive touch, but one of sympathy, an easier, simpler gesture for this Hispanic woman than for any Anglo women I have known. My frailty and failure were acceptable to her, part of my claim on being human. "Sympathy" is too thin a word; Yolanda was *sympatica*.

When I tried to make a joke about the idiocy of my wife's sudden need to liberate herself from the weight of generations, Yolanda raised her index finger and waved it before my eyes. This business of blood and its power and force, this was something she understood. I should not belittle the mother of my child, not for this. It was beneath me to sneer. Yes, the woman was wrong, she could not evade her blood, but perhaps in time she would learn this as even Yolanda had.

Silently, we sipped each other's sadness, a drink less toxic when shared. In the end, Yolanda had been unable to become Puerto Rican enough. Great causes die even as they are embraced. She had drifted from failure to failure.

I said I understood, and she shrugged.

She had been selfless, I had been selfish. Caught in currents neither of us could navigate, we struggled. From opposite shores we had spiraled helplessly toward a common center. There was no escaping the whirlpool. I said as much. I would accomplish nothing of real worth. Writing? Never. My disease was self-absorption; my lot was ruin. I had deceived myself, and by so doing, I destroyed everything I loved.

Did I truly believe what I said, she asked.

I said I did.

Yolanda's eyes grew nearly as wide as they had been in those days when she wore pink plastic spectacles. We could drink more cheaply at her mother's house, she said. We should leave.

"Come with me," she said softly, and when I hesitated she said nothing, but with the touch of three fingers beneath my elbow lifted me from my bar stool.

The apartment was dark; her mother was out. The air in the small rooms smelled of dust and heat trapped an entire July day behind closed windows. They had no air-conditioning. Plastic seat covers made the rented furniture sticky and uncomfortable, so after Yoli poured two glasses of gin over ice, we stepped from our shoes and sat on a musty, thin carpet.

Was what I said in the bar truly how I felt? Is that what I thought? Could I not know I had time and again saved her life, kept her thinking that it was possible to achieve something fine? Even when I had not been there, she had thought of the many things I had taught her, the books, the ideas, all that teacher stuff—did I think it was nothing? They had never been able to convince her of the pervasive evil of the *Yanqui* conquerors because of how I opened my life to her and she learned that she need not be what the street, or her mother, or her school, or her sisters, or the Party, or her husband had said she must be. *Dios.* Ten years teaching, I must have had two thousand students—did I think I affected none of them? *Maestro*, are you that blind?

She was not scolding me. She was not laughing. Life was more complicated than I knew—this is what always puzzled her about *Yanquis*. Why must everything be reduced to a simple equation, every problem have its solution, every solution matched neatly to its problem, when what she knew from the tides that surged in her blood was that nothing was so simple? I was smarter than the average *Yanqui*. For the love of God, it was I who taught her these truths.

She placed my palm on her breast. Her mother would not return for hours. Cooled by the drink she held, Yoli's hand gently touched my throat. She said nothing as she stood. In the half-light, she moved, a zipper rasped, and her black dress fell about her feet.

In her mother's bed, there was no question of lust long delayed, nor could we fabricate any illusion about how this would for us both be the beginning of something new and grand. I would never see her again. There was no debt, but this was payback, a gift drawn from the well of despair. It was all Yolanda had to give, and it was given purely, in the fullness of her heart, given quietly and completely.

In her arms that night, I was granted the grace that comes only with a woman's unqualified compassion. I did not understand her motives then; I am unsure I understand them now. But that night, as I lay beside her, I was renewed. Her fingers entwined in the damp hair at the nape of my neck, and Yolanda held me as though I had returned home to a place where, strangely, I had never before been.

If I Can't Have You
Yvonne Elliman

When Sarah Fernandez dances, there's no ambiguity in her hands, her torso, her generous eyes, fragrant hair, or parted lips. She breathes the words: *If I can't have you, I don't want nobody, baby.* It's the '70s, and by donning a tightly tailored white suit and busting some never-to-be-forgotten moves, John Travolta has metamorphosed from Sweathog to Heir Apparent to Gene Kelly. Call it cooption, call it mainstreaming, Travolta's bony ass persuades white America that an urban dance craze invented by gay men, Hispanics, and blacks must now be a part of every *bar mitzvah*, sweet sixteen and wedding. Out with the Hokey-Pokey, in with the Hustle.

"If I Can't Have You" is only one song off the remarkable soundtrack of *Saturday Night Fever*—lush strings, insistent beat, simple lyrics, the straight up disco that has moved the national barometer off songs of protest and rock guitar-god fury to mindless sweetness and endless electronic loops of synthesized rhythm. The film's origins are a *New York Herald Tribune* Sunday supplement feature about a Brooklyn subculture. At Bay Ridge High School where I worked, disco is last year's local news.

Bay Ridge, Brooklyn, this wellspring of American

pop culture, is the very neighborhood where the Travolta film's story unfolds. I dance with Sarah Fernandez because I am one of several chaperones on the Senior Trip, a journey to a dude ranch in the Poconos. It is difficult to ascertain exactly when ranch hands drove cattle through the gentle hills of eastern Pennsylvania, but there are horses, stables, wagon wheels on the walls, hay, hurricane lamps, rooms in log cabins called bunkhouses, and the food is a buffet of beans, veiny steak and hearty bread.

Back in Brooklyn, Tony Manero wanted something more than to be a paint-store stock clerk on 86th Street. He dances. Geez, how he dances! Master of his world, he is painfully aware it is a small one. He lives with his parents in a row house. Tony's gifts are not intellectual, but that doesn't feel terribly critical, considering that his smarter older brother, a Catholic priest, suffers a crisis of faith. The priest has no ready answers for Tony's friends who turn to him for explanations for their suffering. The priest has no answers for himself. Evidently, intellect is not what all is cracked up to be and suffering cannot be explained away without faith, faith being what the priest knows he lacks. Better to dance.

Tony's sole ambition is to transport his life across the East River to Manhattan, a physical passage far short of any schlep to the Poconos, but a spiritual journey of galactic proportions. *Saturday Night Fever* tells the story of all my high school students; it tells my story. As in the script, most of us lack the courage to take the first step.

To my students, the disco craze is almost passé. As

16 and 17-year olds, they easily pass for 18, the drinking age in an era when anyone fit to tote an M-14 is grudgingly deemed fit to chug a beer. For my young women who easily obtain two or three social security accounts, receive multiple welfare checks, and inflate the count of dependent children at a given address by passing infants up and down rear window fire-escapes any time the Welfare people show up unannounced to count heads, obtaining a mere driver's license with a false birthday presents little challenge. Dance clubs open their doors to them.

Sarah has no designs on me. I hardly know her. Like most Bay Ridge seniors, she is street-legal and more worldly than any 18-year-old should be, but she deigns to dance with me because except for one or two employees, the few male teachers along for the ride are the only people at the ranch with more than legs in their pants. There are no other guests. For the stable-hands, these three days will be a legend that when they recount, no one will believe. *How many girls? How old? Yeah, right.* Pete, Duke, and Eddie show up late for breakfast. They eat steak and eggs and drink pitchers of orange juice. My buddy, Frank, a guidance counselor, says, "They seem a little weak in the knees," and when Lynne, who is nominally in charge of this adventure, says, "Too much time in the saddle," we near choke on our cinnamon toast.

We dance in the ranch's saloon, the only place with a jukebox. With our visit, being the sole guests, the saloon is alcohol-free, but that presents no obstacle to intoxication: our girls swig contraband tequila, rum, and wine in their rooms, or they smoke Puerto Rican lettuce out in some dark field before they head for the dance floor. Sarah's molten chocolate eyes glow with the inner heat of Ron Rico and Coca-Cola.

Sarah wears a short swirling dress run with red and green and yellow and blue thread, open-toe platform shoes with leather straps that lace to her knees, a filmy mostly visible crimson bra, and a translucent sleeveless white blouse, unbuttoned, but tied into a loose bow near her waist. The rings on her fingers are set with all manner of colored stones, and a gold clasp gathers the scarlet scarf at her neck. Bobby-pinned purple wild flowers flutter above her ears. When the beat suggests it, she entwines her fingers in her long, loose, black hair and her slender, pale arms pile it over her head where she releases it to fall over her face and back. Shaking free of the tangle, she laughs as she turns, reaches for my hand, and spins me twice in place while she claps her hands like a flamenco dancer.

She knows I am inept. She leads.

I thought I could dance, but that three days I learn that "dancing" is not the word for what I do. I was capable of a creditable version of the White Boy Shuffle by trying something with an overbite to show intensity, raising my fists to shoulder height, and rhythmically shrugging my shoulders. Inspired, I might do a 360-degree turn. This performance won me praise at Jewish weddings. Occasionally, I'd risk lifting a foot from the floor.

But my black and Latina kids move in ways that are

an order apart. Never confuse dancing with the mob aerobics at white clubs induced by modest amounts of X, cocaine, or Special K, deafening sound, laser lights, and smoke machines that have otherwise sane people jumping like pogo sticks. My high school students understood dancing to be about the glories of the body, sex standing up with some of your clothes on, clothes donned not for propriety, but to enhance the suggestion of what lay beneath. Done right, social dancing suggests carnality with no messy obligations to deliver anything beyond a smile, a wink, and, perhaps, a finger that curls along a partner's cheek. The line from *Saturday Night Fever* that rings truest is when Travolta derides a female partner by saying, "If you fuck like you dance…" and shakes his head with scorn and pity.

My high school girls danced from the ankles up. They had joints in their hips and spines unknown to any anatomy chart. Their ease and acceptance of their own bodies was breathtaking and, to my white-boy eyes, revelatory.

Years later, it makes me think. During my ten years at an all girls' high school, I never met an anorexic kid. Not one. Asceticism is a disease peculiar to white girls engaged in denial of their physicality.

Someone is sure to call me a racist for suggesting that black and Hispanic kids make better dancers and are probably more relaxed at sex, from which it must follow that I also believe black kids cannot have the ability to become corporate presidents. I harbor no such feelings. We'd all be better off if the CEOs of the

Fortune 500 could bust a move good as Sarah. It is worth noting, however, that the white side of the racial divide in America is not only in denial of its own sexuality, but is terrified and fascinated by the sexuality the other side seems to enjoy.

Put plain, white people are tight-assed and frightened of people who are not.

Whenever a dance fad bubbles upward from the projects or the barrio—the Hustle or the Lambada, or, further back, the Tango or Mambo, or The Charleston or the odiously named Black Bottom—for a short while, otherwise respectable white folk will hazard a bump and a grind, hands will caress a partner's torso, and a few white guys will get laid in new ways, perhaps by their wives. However, after a brief hormonal flush and a national flirtation with sensuality, we'll return to flapping our elbows and it will Mashed Potato Time all over again.

Dirty Dancing, that newly acclaimed film classic with its startling soundtrack, underscores the point. "Dirty" dancers touch—that's why they are dirty. A nice Jewish girl named "Baby" comes of age in the Catskills in 1963 by embracing the physicality of sensuous dance and Patrick Swayze's pert tush. Beauty not only learns to embrace the Beast, but to do a split and lift to the lyrics of "I've Had the Time of My Life." While Mickey and Sylvia sizzle on "Love Is Strange" with its Latino cha-cha rhythm, at the film's core is a morality play: unleashed passion leads to pregnancy and death when an illegal abortion nearly kills a dancer. White girls who dance dirty flirt with ruin.

Terror goes out of control when the unleashed sexuality is male; instead of self-inflicted starvation, untrammeled male sexuality requires violence. Men who beat the crap out of gay men are propelled by their dread of penetration, a fear rooted in the haunting suspicion, *What if I like it?* In this twisted thinking, like measles or flu, homosexuality is a contagion to be avoided at all costs. A single exposure to homosexual sex—outside of prisons, that is—will make a fag a fag for life. Queers need stomping because homosexual sex, untrammeled male sexuality, is so potent it can spread like wildfire. We can't allow that shit to happen. No way. Hit the fucker with a tire iron.

Oh, sure, white folk dance. They also box, run hurdles, and play basketball—just not terribly well. It's easy to speculate about the icy climates in which Anglo-Saxon habits first formed the pathetic, eternal effort to control, master, posses, conquer and subdue anything and everything, but at the end I am left as bewildered as anyone on the origins of the predisposition to hate.

What I do know is that at a cowboy dude ranch in the Poconos, Sarah Fernandez worried about none of this. She did not worry about racial differences. She did not worry why people were as stupid as they were. She just moved. She looked damned fine doing it, too. Sarah Fernandez knew what we too easily forget: the best parts of life—joy, sex, children—are not executive perquisites, cost not a dime, and take place below the neck.

—for Gladys Molina

Stairway to Heaven
Led Zeppelin

Anita Marie for a year sat in my high school Junior Honors Creative Writing class, period five every day, first seat, first row. She laughed frequently and easily, at herself as much as anyone else, and she had a bizarre associative mind that gleefully identified the ridiculous in anything—anti-drug "rap" sessions conducted by middle-aged New York City apparatchiks who could not recognize the aroma of marijuana; History classes assigned to students who spoke no English; our tone-deaf Music & Orchestra teacher too vain or too far into denial to wear a hearing aid. Anita Marie was partial to dark colors, the fashion of the time, but my mind insists on remembering her with some sort of eyelet lace collar.

 A fair complexioned African-American girl, her hair was by red rubber bands bound into short pigtails, and she wore very little make-up, no more than a touch of lip-gloss. Her smile could charm Stalin from the Kremlin, and that smile most often danced on her lips when she spoke about Rat, her Puerto Rican grocery-clerk lover. That, she insisted, was the boy's name. He was Rat, and Rat could be known by no other name. When Anita Marie wrote a breathless prose tribute to the wonder of his eyes and the marvels of his hands and shoulders, the flatness of his abdomen and smoothness of his forearms, in all the hormonal enthusiasm of her sixteen years, with little notion of the language's resonance and potential, she began with four simple words: "Rat worked the Meat." That placed him at the deli counter, all right, but by her sly smile, I knew she understood her words suggested a little more.

I never knew Anita Marie really well, so I'm clueless as to why one hot July night she and Rat ran a garden hose from the exhaust pipe to the passenger compartment of his rusted Toyota. They were found in each other's arms, gray with death.

Michael hanged himself. At the New England college where I taught for a decade, Michael was an effeminate vortex of need who regaled everyone within earshot about that on-going disaster, this marvelous *opéra bouffe,* his life. Nothing ordinary ever happened to Michael. Nothing. In a mere two hours, he could relate the most in*cred*ible, a*maz*ing, un*like*ly details of a thirty-minute trip to the convenience store, incontrovertible evidence of how the universe conspired to amuse, frustrate, educate, and entertain him. He was a brilliant mimic; his stories spared no ethnic accent, no gesture or mannerism. Michael's hair went from green to gold to white to blue and back to green, but one spring afternoon when the boy *de jour* spurned his avowals of eternal devotion, Michael underestimated the force of a melodramatic gesture when he looped his belt over the steam pipe that ran across his dorm room ceiling, climbed atop a chair and kicked himself into Eternity. He botched it, of course, failing to break his neck, and so was found strangling and kicking. Frantic efforts did not save him. It took Michael several days to die of the brain damage he suffered from oxygen deprivation brought on by asphyxiation.

And there was Beth, a certified schizophrenic lesbian whose parents had sufficient wealth to pay and pay and pay again for the readmission and rematriculation of their only daughter to Drake University, the expensive private school in the Midwest where Beth enrolled in a loosely structured course of study she herself designed. She studied nothing; she studied everything. During her less lucid intervals, Beth was consigned to a discreet mental institution; *The Bin*, Beth called it. Maybe the two campuses looked alike. I would not know about that. But I knew, because Beth told me, that Beth loved love, to be in love, and especially to be falling in love anew.

She could disarm you with a glance and a question. After confessing her fascination with women's muscled arms, Beth once leaned across a campus cafeteria table and with her index finger moved her auburn hair from over her eyes to ask me which features of female anatomy made me turn my head. *She's a stranger*, said Beth, *and she's strolling toward you in the mall. You'll never see her again. She's absolutely unaware of you. Come on, Perry, what exact part do you watch as she goes by?*

Beth was happiest in her off-campus apartment writing dozens of tiny Post-It notes to be found by her lover. "Treasure Hunt," she called her game, and at the end of the trail of rhyming clues there were tulips and chocolate-covered stemmed cherries and Beth herself, each prize, including Beth, suitably gift-wrapped in green ribbons and yellow cellophane.

Because during my years at Drake I was the sole parent of a nine-year-old girl, I frequently held class in my living room, an arrangement that not only lessened childcare problems, but also made me something of a campus resource. It was commonplace for my students to drop by; as often as not they found other students had done the same. Beth found her way to that living room at odd hours. If vodka and lithium do not mix, Beth had not heard. One night, at an hour when the good people of the Midwestern plains were long asleep and dreaming their good dreams, Beth showed me the crosshatched cuttings she'd sliced with a serrated steak knife on her smoother skin below her bicep. The wounds still oozed, and as she pressed the bath towel I gave her over what looked like a blood-etched chessboard, she told me she had maybe skipped some meds, did I think she was in trouble?

Six months later, Beth was dead by her own hand. She had once more been in residence at the Bin, so none of us who knew her as a student had any inkling as to how or what or precisely when Beth had done what Beth did. We knew only that Beth who loved love was irrevocably gone.

They leave me blue, my suicides, but they also leave me very, very angry. I don't know what to do with my anger. There is no one to shout at, no one to shake, no one to lecture, no one to improve, no one to challenge, no one to motivate, no one to inspire, no one to receive any of the ministrations a teacher is prepared to deliver.

If you're middle-aged as I am, on the grimmest nights all you know is the opportunities missed, the paths not taken, the indiscretion you wished you had had the courage—or stupidity—to commit, and so you wonder how anyone still gifted with youth could discard so much sheer opportunity.

Now, occasionally some lunatic demonstrates that the Devil implants self-destructive suggestions on recordings played backwards. Most of us cannot make out the words going forward, but these prophets inspired by the Lord testify that "Stairway to Heaven" played in reverse says, "I sing because I live with Satan." This powerful, if somewhat dyslexic, suggestion has it that Led Zeppelin is league with The Lord of the Flies in a plot to rob an adolescent of his will, seek out a weapon, and after killing everyone in sight then spatter his own brains onto a school building wall.

Potent stuff, that rock 'n roll.

The self-appointed guardians of American values find demonic explanations far easier to accept than any notion that the consumer culture in which they submerge suburban youth may be less than spiritually fulfilling. First note that inner city kids, living where weaponry is easier to obtain and life presumably harder, never find life to be all that bleak. The Devil prefers the souls of mall-children. Mall-children know their future will be about malls, shopping in malls, working in malls, driving in traffic to get to malls, growing up to make and sell the stuff sold in malls . It's not the American Dream; it's the American Nightmare. Is it any wonder they are not delirious with joy?

There are plenty of other theories. Maybe my suicides are flotsam in the wake of divorce, or the result of a million mind-numbing hours of television, or perhaps they are the consequences of careless lives consumed by sex, drugs, and rock 'n roll. Maybe they have been bullied into suicide by a bazillion hours of computer games that lead them to believe that after they release a fusillade of bullets someone will press a Holy Reset Button so they might be reborn to a heroic new life. Maybe kids need an unequivocal spiritual center, regular church attendance, tough love, and better hygiene; maybe they need less Prozac, vitamins, clean mountain air, colonics, less sugar, no Internet, and daily calisthenics.

I don't believe any of it. Not a word.

I know only that at some point my Anitas and Michaels and Beths preferred Ending to Struggle. With their foreheads placed against a blank, gray concrete wall of insignificance, their eyes were open wide, but for the lack of imagination we failed to instill in them they believed the blank grayness inches from their eyes extending featureless forever away was all there was and all that ever would be. Achievement and change were never in sight. Struggle led only to more struggle. They could not imagine change, much less victory.

Decades of teaching, yet I have no program, no wisdom, not even a prayer to offer for my Anitas and Michaels and Beths. I have nothing but the sodden weight of my failure.

My Anitas and Michaels and Beths are dead. Nothing else. They are nothing more. They are nothing less. They will never be other than what they are or were. The pathetic little memorials of stuffed animals, heaped flowers, white plastic crosses, cards that read, "We Remember" scrawled in crayon set beneath a smiling photo in a $3.98 faux-wood frame purchased in haste at Wal-Mart, these trappings of grief are soon swept away.

My Anitas and Michaels and Beths are not elevated to sainthood, they are not called to be among angels. They heed no summons to God, they are vouchsafed no Divine vision. They know no final flash of cosmic wisdom. They are not unfulfilled potential, they are not saved innocents, they are not victims, they are not martyrs, they are not even remembered.

My Anitas and Michaels and Beths are dead. Dead. Just goddam dead.

I'm Free
The Who

My first pregnant student is Vivian, a little bit of a thing, 17, with a voice like cashmere and a face full and simple as a Tintoretto. Since Vivian has a gap in her daily schedule at the same time I do, she meets with me in the English office to help mark my papers and assist with clerical work. I ignore the admonition never to be alone with a student behind a closed door, and my daring is rewarded by her humor, confidence, loyalty and companionship.

One afternoon, she boosts herself up to sit on the desk before me and undoes her belt. "I'm getting fat," she says. She undoes her waistband. The zipper of her jeans slips a few inches, exposing the red embroidery thread that runs through the elastic waistband of her white cotton underwear. "I'm really getting fat," she repeats, patting her abdomen.

I look into the deep, black expressive pools of her eyes, and never consider that the kid unzipping her fly could possibly be doing anything but making a pass at me. I hastily gather my papers and bolt from the room. I am 21; everything, everywhere, was about me.

Three weeks later, Vivian vanishes. She does not quit school; she just disappears.

Francis tells me Vivian is "preggers." They sat beside

each other in my last class of the day, a class of tracked "commercial juniors," a designation that indicates they have no college ambitions, but strive to become accomplished typists equally adept at Gregg and Pitman shorthand. No one yet types on a computer. No one yet is an administrative assistant. This is Brooklyn, New York, in the early '70s, and across the river in the corporate offices of Manhattan where the twin towers of the World Trade Center have just risen to gleam taller than the other buildings of the skyline, a skilled secretary commands a better salary than a mere school teacher.

Francis, I swear, looks like Betty from *Archie Comics*. A fair 19-year-old Italian kid, she chews pencils, wears pale jeans with rolled cuffs, men's white shirts with sleeves too long, has her genuinely blonde hair cut to a pageboy or tied into a ponytail. Francis could be the last bobby-soxer in America except that rather than scream herself into a hysterical faint for Frank Sinatra, Francis faints for Paul McCartney. She writes class assignments while sitting on the unpolished wooden floor with her legs propped above her on a classroom wall. Though they prefer desks, none of her classmates thinks this unusual, and I see no harm in it. If I had met Francis anywhere else, I'd have confessed my age and dated her, or at least have tried. Fact is, Francis would have found me insufficiently sophisticated and turned me down flat.

In that triple-shift overcrowded school, the final class of the day starts at 4:00 and purportedly ends at 4:38, but the thirty-two girls in the class pretty much decide their education ends at 4:15 at which time they dump compacts, hairbrushes, mascara, blush, and eyeliner from bulging pocketbooks to their desks to prepare themselves for their imminent departure. For the following fifteen minutes, six or seven go to the windows to point out which guy in which car awaits each of them. Fresh Dentyne is passed all around. The thick aroma of cosmetics fills my classroom. English class? Oh, sure, Mr. G., any day now.

I admit that discussing the relative charms of Tony or Eduardo or Felipe supersedes anything I might have to say about *A Tale of Two Cities*, the novel I am mandated to teach, but I feel a sense of professional pride: I mean, *Geez*, I am supposed to teach *something*, right? So in what maybe my first inspired moment as a teacher, I cut a deal: in the teacher's wooden coat closet at the back of the room is a full-length mirror. I will unlock the closet door at 4:30 and allow use of that mirror—but not until 4:30. Everyone agrees this is reasonable. I concede eight minutes to recoup fifteen, while their lives, which are about future office jobs and the young men who loiter outside, remain uncomplicated by Charles Darnay and Lucie Manette.

But that stenographer's life will never be Vivian's. When Francis delivers the news, she is matter-of-fact. Careless girls get knocked up. *Where is she?* "The Bronx somewhere," Francis calls back to me over her shoulder as she dashes down the hall, a blue looseleaf notebook clutched to her chest.

I conducted five classes with near 170 students that first semester. It was difficult to keep track. I was young, I was inexperienced, I was stupid.

Was Vivian trying to get me to talk about it? What might have been different had I asked the right questions? Had given the advice? Where is Vivian now? In what Bronx walk-up did she peddle her ass for rent money? Youth and self-absorption made me miss something; I still feel the gap like a new space between my teeth.

Temptation sat at every classroom desk, but Bay Ridge High School also offered me heady virtue. One morning in May after I have taught for a few years, I notice Lois in a sweatshirt. Outside, the sun fires the city to more than 90 degrees; the school's halls are a ceramics oven. New York City abandoned trying to enforce dress codes, so the girls wear next to nothing; they glory in their bodies, take every opportunity to wear translucent shirts, shorts, T-shirts, nothing but silk kerchiefs tied around their chests, their hard midriffs bare. Isn't this the advantage of attending a single sex school? A girl can dress comfortably and no one will care. OK, maybe the young, male teacher will notice, but jiggling a little bare flesh in front of a teacher is nothing more than good fun, safe practice for the real thing.

But on a day when a brassiere is as common as white tuxedoes at a tractor pull, here is Lois, dressed for football practice in Green Bay. She perspires so freely that her gray sweatshirt wetly sticks between her shoulder blades. You could wring it out to fill a coffee cup.

Lois, a genuinely smart kid who never misses her

homework, spread the word how on another day, my new wife, Helena, enjoyed an ice cream cone while waiting for me on the school's front steps when Lois sat beside her. Lois thought Helena was a new student. When they straightened that out, they shared a good laugh, and Helena offered her a lick. *The white lady offered me a lick of her ice cream!* The story gets around, and among the girls I have that much more juice.

Lois was a tall, easy smiling kid, maybe 5' 11", from Panama, the Canal Zone, where her father, a sergeant or something, had died when Lois could not yet walk. Her mother was a native Panamanian who'd come to Nueva York and remarried.

That May, the air is thick as petroleum jelly. It should have been August. Each morning we breathe the same foul atmosphere as the day before. A dome of poisonous air called a Bermuda High is suspended over the city like a tent, trapping the soot, smoke and carcinogenic fumes that emerge from the ass-end of every truck, bus, and car in town. We live in a polluted pressure cooker, but every day here is Lois in the same gray sodden sweatshirt.

So after school that afternoon, I follow Lois and a few other kids down the granite steps and into the street. My car is parked around the corner, but I follow her as if by accident. We stroll to the subway stop. It is nothing but luck when the student group breaks up and Lois steps alone into a corner candy store. I buy cigarettes. She says, "Hi," as she tries to pass me near the register. I say, "I have to ask you, Lo'; why the sweatshirt?"

She looks as if I have gut-stuck her. Lois makes me swear I will tell no one, not even her good buddy, my wife. Right there near the comic book rack, Lois rolls up her sleeves and shows me the welts up and down her forearms, angry purple lines in her dark flesh that stand out maybe a quarter of an inch, some crusted with scabs, and some moist and red as freshly broken fruit.

"What the hell is that?" I ask, already sick with knowing.

Outside, palpable heat rises from the pavement. We walk a bit. Then in a rush, Lois, who has arms like Pearl Bailey and likes to laugh and eat vanilla ice cream more than do anything else, tells me about her stepfather whose new game is to whip on Lois with an automobile antenna he keeps in a closet specifically for that purpose. Now Lois may be 25 in her body, but she is no more than 15 in her head. The puzzlement behind her eyes is as painful as the wounds on her arms and Christ knows where else. No, her mother didn't know what was going on, but Lois is sure the woman will blame her. She always did. And no, her stepfather hadn't raped her yet, but she was sure that was coming; she just hoped he wouldn't make her do anything disgusting. Terror made her linger near the school until it closed instead of traveling by subway with her friends. Lois is in no hurry to get home. She tells me she rides trains until ten or eleven or later, even through the night until sun-up, preferring the danger below New York City's streets to the certain peril of her own home. She bathes in the school's long dysfunctional gymnasium showers, choosing a quick spray of rusted cold water to being naked anywhere else.

Laws requiring teachers to report abuse did not yet exist. Still, I tell Lois I must tell someone.

She cries. Revealing her secret to me, she had been fine, but now her face dissolves into a runny mess. We return to the luncheonette where I buy her vegetable soup. Then we slowly walk back to the school and I telephone Lefky, my high school buddy recently out of law school who now works for the City's Corporation Council. His name is really Lefkowitz, of course, but it is possible his own mother calls him Lefky.

I tell Lefky Lois's story. Most of it, anyway. Lefky, a practical man, believes Lois shows good sense not wanting to have the son-of-a-bitch arrested. The kid would have to testify, and until the trial came around she'd need an injunction to keep him away, but those things never work. Any injunction requested by an abused woman, Lefky tells me, is a pre-death certificate if she has no means to escape her environment. Lois's best outcome, Lefky tells me, will be to be placed into a foster home, hardly a day at the beach. For sure, to disappear into the system, she will have to change high schools.

When I say, "That sucks," Lefky says, "Why doesn't she have herself declared an independent minor?"

I've never heard of this. Lefky explains the strategy to create a legal status that will allow Lois to move out of her mother's house and into her own place with welfare money from the City to keep body and soul together until she finishes high school. "The kid will have to file papers, but in a few months..."

I look at Lois standing nearby and I recall the welts on her arms. "No, she needs something now," I say. "We're talking life and death, here, Lefk."

Lefky earns a bottle of single malt scotch when he says, "Is she there? Put the kid on," and takes thirty minutes worth of information from Lois. Lefky personally walks the papers through an office on the floor below his own, and, three days later, after a quick appearance before a judge during his lunch hour, the city cuts Lois an emergency check. Within hours, Lois and a welfare worker are looking for a place for Lois to live. She can talk about vanilla ice cream all she wants, but I ask her to keep this one to herself.

I think she went to the University of Connecticut where, amazingly, the ghetto girl from Panama rowed crew; those tree-trunk legs would have been noticed by any sharp-eyed coach eyeballing first-year students getting off the bus.

That's the last I heard.

I suppose I could have followed the rules, involved a counselor, maybe the police, and never made a phone call.

I could have done it that way.

Rules are rules, right?

Pat was in my Sophomore Modified English class. A kid could land in the Modified track for any number of reasons, the most common being stupidity. Since stupidity precipitates any number of "other" hostile behaviors, and since *slow* was okay, but *disruptive* a pain in the ass, a well-behaved stupid kid more likely would be maintained in the Regular track while a disruptive kid would be cast down into Modified, a far shore from which no student ever returned.

Maintaining order was the only criterion for a teacher's success with the Modified group, and order meant not much more than keeping them out of the hallways. They were free to assault each other and eat books and chalk so long as chaos did not spill into other classrooms. They were mostly black and from foreign countries — Haiti, Jamaica, or Mississippi, three distant lands totally alien to Brooklyn. It may be that school systems have a predisposition to see people of color as troublesome, or it may be that people of color live in poorer neighborhoods because of wider racism, but whatever the cause, in that Modified classroom, Pat stood out like a snowflake on black velvet.

Half-Polish and half-Irish with a shock of blond hair that must have been hacked with a knife, Pat spent her time with her face cradled on her arms. She had a bad case of acne. I was cruising around the room reading aloud when as I passed her desk I bent to ask if she were all right. "Fucking A," she mumbled. "Crashing?" I asked and she weakly waved her hand. I said, "Sleep," and touched the back of her neck as you might a kitten's (a gesture that today would drop me into an abyss of grief, pain and personal liability).

The very next semester, Pat was assigned to no fewer than three of my classes — my left-back 9th graders, my Remedial Reading class, and the second half of the Sophomore Modified class in which I'd first met her, a class that she needed to repeat. She did not hold it against me that I had failed her with an attendance code grade of 49. My high school classes had at least 32 students, even Remedial Reading where the highest reading score was barely adequate to the 6th grade. We had no specialized materials. Dutifully, I distributed hard cover copies of *Silas Marner*. My kids pawned their books for the weight of the paper. They'd claim their texts were stolen or lost; I'd issue them a new book; they'd sell that in turn. In this way, semesters came and went, booksellers grew wealthy, and in some very dark recess of some very obscure room in a little known sub-basement of the Board of Education, a bureaucrat earned a salary by tallying lost books against properly filled out receipts.

Pat's academic advisor explained to me that Pat requested to be assigned to as many classes of mine as possible because she trusted me. On Pat's abbreviated schedule, that amounted to three out of her five classes each day, an illegal arrangement, but one the counselor hoped might induce Pat to abandon truancy as a way of life. I was not the only subversive at Bay Ridge High School.

The plan worked, in a modified way. Pat showed up as many as four days per week once she realized that she could attend one of my classes, not appear in the other two, and still suffer no consequences; I preferred strangulation with a piano wire to filing the forms required by the school's Discipline Police. None of those kids was being scared into coming to class by an attendance officer. The vast apparatus that made daily attendance part of the formula of how state and federal aid was doled out to city schools, not to mention how welfare payments were paid out to individuals, was a machine for which I refused to be a cog.

So Pat and I became friends. For Pat, school supplied a free hot breakfast, free lunch, several drug-free hours, and warmth in winter. No one expected her to attend the two other classes of her five-period daily schedule, both of which were Physical Education. I don't think she could have found the school gym with a map and a compass. But as long as she was assured that in Mr. G's classroom she could sleep off whatever illegal substance flowed through her system, she came to school when it suited her. Safer than the subway, it smelled better, too. Why not?

Pat was brighter than anyone knew. I created some bogus assignment to gather writing samples, and while her class industriously carved their ballpoint pens into lined paper, Pat in a delicate hand that bespoke Catholic school and early penmanship lessons wrote the lyrics of "I'm Free" from memory. It's one of the sweeter songs from the Who's *Tommy, the Rock Opera*.

I'm free,
I am free,
And freedom tastes of reality.

This was 1972, and rapport was automatic between a desperate kid and the hippie-freak teacher. America was still being greened; I was a sprout in the cracked pavement.

Eventually, Pat vanished. It was not easy to notice.

Pat not appearing for a few days was hardly cause for alarm, but after a while I missed our conversations on the cosmic timbre of Grace Slick's voice and allusive meaning in the lyrics of The Grateful Dead. Pat had persuaded me that *Uncle John's Band* was about John the Baptist. It was disappointing not to see her for several weeks.

Then her father showed up.

The guy wore a rumpled gray suit too tight around his gut, but nevertheless buttoned. He was short, powerfully built, roseate in his face, and he leaned forward like a game pit bull. His knuckles whitened against my desktop as he loomed over me and asked, "Where's my kid?" I asked which was his. He barked his last name and dropped into the oak chair beside my desk. He propped his head on his fist, and leaned toward me to repeat his name. We were old buddies, we were. Men of the world. Partners in some sort of private knowledge. He exhaled cheap whiskey. His badly knotted red tie was clipped to his white shirt by the Marine Corps Globe and Eagle. *Semper Fi*. The Vietnam War was still being waged on the evening news, so his war would have been Korea.

I told him I had not seen Pat in some time and was sorry to know he had not, either. That much was true. He went into a muttered rant about ingratitude, how Pat was worse than her mother had ever been, God rest the faithless bitch. He itemized on his thick fingers all the things he'd done for Pat. There was food, clothing, and shelter. That shit cost. And there were the times she was sick. Goddam doctor bills. Goddam doctors.

He got as far as eight fingers. It takes longer to read this than it took to occur. He was up and gone out my classroom door before I could say much of anything at all.

Days later, Cookie, a Dominican girl whose real name was something unpronounceable for me, told me that everyone knew Pat had gone off with her boyfriend, a guy who owned a motorcycle, and they were probably already in California.

I marveled at that. At the grand old age of 24, nailed into teaching to maintain my draft deferment, flight was something about which I could only dream. *Easy Rider* was new, Scott McKenzie's *If You Go to San Francisco*, the hymn to a celestial Haight-Ashbury everyone knew never existed, was only a few years old. Transcontinental flight is America's most enduring romance.

But at that time, mainstream America was dimly recognizing that immolating Asian children created dissonances that drove their own children insane. The war was coming home. A generation was so convinced their parents were idiots that they were perpetually stoned and living in communes. Cautionary tales of runaway teenagers encountering and succumbing to depravity and death were in high demand. It was old news at Bay Ridge High School, though. My inner city girls had been fucked, drugged, abused, and abandoned for years and years, but now that suburban sons were returning from the jungle addicted to black tar heroin and their white sisters at home were selling their bodies to purchase chemical oblivion, the national consciousness acknowledged evil stalked the land.

You saw the fear in checkout-aisle magazines. *Will*

Your Daughter Suddenly Be Gone? Martin Scorcese filmed *Taxi Driver*, the movie in which Harvey Keitel pimps out a 12-year-old Jodie Foster who kneels to give Robert DeNiro head before he flips out on a blood-soaked killing spree. I wrote my first published short story about a runaway and an addled arsonist. The unequivocal sign America is in the shit is a TV movie, and there were several made about teenage runaways. The 30-second promos promised daring glimpses of quivering teenage flesh, and only incidentally also sold ads for soap, cars, and beer. Such entertainment always ended with an uplifting redemptive message.

One movie told the honest-to-God true story of a New York City priest whose entire adolescent congregation peddled their asses between 42nd and 48th Streets, the so-called "Minnesota Strip" on Eighth Avenue. It seems that Middle American runaways, male or female, alighted in Manhattan's Port Authority Bus Terminal and were sucking dick before they could buy a Twinkie. When the spunky girl with dark hair dies of an overdose, the priest persuades her blond friend to drop a dime and call home where her tearful parents promised to be more attentive—maybe by taking their daughter on a shopping spree, pick up a new outfit, spend a few dollars, feel good in approved ways. Maybe Dad even promises to stop doing his daughter. I don't recall how realistic the movie was, but as is usual with Pop culture, the blonde is redeemed while the dark girl serves as an object lesson.

But as Cookie delivered the news about Pat's departure, and even today, despite the genuine risks of running off, I thought Pat was right to take her chances. The best shot she had at a life was escape.

See, I'd met her old man.

Good sense tells me she was abandoned in some truck stop no farther west than Gary, Indiana, but in this case good sense and my reflexive cynicism do not prevail. I choose to remember what was unlikely. I cannot hear the guitar chords of any song from *Tommy* without thinking of Pat, of course, and the image I carry of her is one I never saw.

Her skinny arms circle the waist of a faceless guy in a black leather jacket. She wears soft brown leather boots and her feet are hard against two chrome pegs. She leans against his shoulder, her cheek against his back. She's 16 years old, free.

After ten years, the bone-grinding desperation of my students' lives drained every illusion I had about my effectiveness as a force for good. I had walked into my very first semester's classes with the Woodstock Festival of Music and Art barely a month in the past, so my career began with my sharing a common youth culture with my students—we were hippies together in spirit if not in dress. But by the decade's end, my students were disco queens, and I was a dinosaur. I no longer understood them. For every Lois I might save, there would be a hundred Vivians missed, a thousand Pats unnoticed.

I signed yearbooks, *Think. Grow. Be. Love easily and well if not wisely*, while I myself was doing none of that. I was idling while toxins spilled from my liver to thicken in my soul. Days, weeks, months, and years passed, but my life was on hold.

The Vietnam draft had seduced me into being a teacher, but once that war was over, I could no longer deceive myself into believing that I compromised to find a way I might avoid being killed while I shed light. No, I was a man standing beneath a cataract trying to strike a match.

I knew I had overstayed my time as a high school teacher when I grew inured to atrocities. Sexual abuse, pregnancy, beatings, drug addiction, rape—really, so what else was new? I might transform to one of those thick-skinned lizards I detested, sunning myself on the granite rock of a union contract, my pension swelling fat while faceless students expired before my half-lidded eyes.

Pat had done right. I did not fear for her. I marveled at her courage.

The Who's final ghostly refrain resonated in my head:

> *How can we follow?*
> *How can we follow?*
> *How can we follow?*

Soon enough, I did.

STILL LOOKING

Love Has No Pride
Bonnie Raitt

In late 1974, in the darkened mezzanine of Radio City Music Hall, I sat between my wife and my lover. Bonnie Raitt had the better seat, on stage on a simple three-legged stool. Raitt took us through "Love Has No Pride," a tune one part gravel to two parts tears. In the shadows beyond the puddle of her spotlight, lurked a guy named Freebo accompanying her on a Fender Fretless bass. On my left, my fingers laced with those of my three-month pregnant wife. On my right, Judith, the first genuine love of my life, quietly wept. I was 26.

    I suppose this should be a confession, but I can find no guilt. The Correctness Cops would require this paragraph to be about recrimination, regret, and apology, but they will be disappointed. I will write no *mea culpas*. These events are pre-'80s, the pitiless decade during which feminist sensibilities cast men who wrote tales about the heterosexual male experience off the Lifeboat of Art while pulling aboard cohorts of women whose tales of promiscuity enabled by the chemical separation of sex and pregnancy were pronounced "liberated." Today, a tale that begins with a phrase like, "genuine love of my life" precipitates a snort of derision if uttered by a man, though pages about women who throw over their lives in search of "fulfillment" are avidly read and admired. A man writing about his infidelity is a braggart shitheel who needs to be excoriated; a woman writing about her infidelity, kinky sex, promiscuity, and deserting her children in search of spiritual and physical nourishment has committees showering her with grant money, has movie rights sold pre-publication, and is sure to be interviewed by an awestruck Matt Lauer. In a thousand arid library meeting rooms, members of the Reading Club will sigh at their heroine-author's courage.

Men pursue pussy while women pursue fulfillment. Everyone knows that. If they should happen to meet in each other's beds, that is an unfortunate accident of biology.

Look, I am a *mensche.* The word is Yiddish and means more than *male.* It means being decent, forthright, and responsible. Being a *mensche* is simple, if not easy.

Protect the weak and do not lie for advantage.

After a million years of evolution, you suddenly want a *mensche* should be *faithful?*

Someone will ask, *Yeah, but what about your wife, asshole? What about her feelings?*

My marriage to Helena was a strong, committed partnership lacking all heat. It would have been an ideal relationship if we had been planning to open a hardware store, shoe store, or maybe greeting cards. We liked and admired each other, and we thought each other pleasant company. We still do.

In our youth, we shared a mission: to live well and

be unconventional. We confused that with passion for each other.

After our honeymoon, in twelve years we never vacationed—not once. Why risk being alone together in a place where we knew no one else?

Marriage had been my mother's idea. When Helena's 20th birthday loomed, just 20 myself and still in college, I noodled what might make an appropriate gift. A dime bag of marijuana might have suited her best, and I was thinking "sweater," but my mother had schemes for my room; she required a spare closet. She said, "Buy her a ring." Helena and I had been dating for three years. "Shit or get off the pot. What are you waiting for?" my mother asked. "It's not fair to her," she added.

What good boy argues with his mother?

Five years after we married, we sat in the dim mezzanine of Radio City Music Hall while Bonnie Raitt sang "Love Has No Pride."

I do not treat adultery lightly. Before you read about The Great Romance, you need to revisit the '70s.

In 1974 when I sat in dim light between my lover and my wife, *fulfillment* and *options* were the newly discovered perquisites of life, newest in the lives of young women who were the first generation in human history to have sex and pregnancy safely and chemically separated. Fidelity was never part of the Aquarian Age. The *human potential* movement was being birthed with primal screams; people terrified by all that freedom paid good money for est training, allegedly a life-altering couple of sessions that pursued individual enlightenment by having enrollees forced to sit long hours cross-legged on a hard floor to be berated by kindly fascists who disallowed them access to a lavatory where they might pee at will.

In 1974, Fritz Perls shaped the *zeitgeist*. Fritz prayed:

I do my thing and you do your thing.
I am not in this world to live up to your expectations,
And you are not in this world to live up to mine.
You are you, and I am I, and if by chance we find
    each other, it's beautiful.
If not, it can't be helped.

Rough translation: "I'm OK, but tough shit if you ain't."

Ecstasy was the nation's obsession. Magazines discovered "the big O," serious, intelligent women rejected their children because motherhood was limiting, Erica Jong pursued and glorified the zipless fuck. With the connection between sex and pregnancy forever broken, fucking, like stamp collecting, became a national hobby. It was risk-free. Back alley abortionists were put out of business in 1973 when Roe vs. Wade was decided in favor of Roe. When in 1969 Dr. David Reuben published *Everything You Always Wanted to Know About Sex (But Were Afraid to Ask)*, it wasn't a Woody Allen punch line. Tupperware Ladies dumped their inventory and transformed their living rooms to bazaars where they sold Ben-Wa balls, edible panties, and vibrators. Anyone who could sit cross-legged studied the *Kama Sutra* and kundalini-yoga with intention of cultivating a three-hour orgasm. Busloads of housewives queued up for tickets to "Deep Throat," the 1972 film with the premise that Linda Lovelace had been born with her clitoris in her throat. They stood on line with Norman Mailer, Truman Capote and Johnny Carson. Helen Gurley Brown, the editor of *Cosmopolitan*, claimed ejaculate was good for the complexion. Porno chic and Nehru jackets were fashionable. Screw baseball; the national pastime had become, well, screwing.

So this meditation will not be a confession, a defense, nor a lament. It is neither apology nor boast. Correctness Cops who demand Glasser stay in line with an appropriate act of penance will be disappointed. Instead, let me take you to a time when betrayal was impossible and self-denial was a symptom of illness, a time when growth meant exploration, when lovers sought to discover joy.

Intoxicating romance and a hormonal surge may have always existed, but in the '70s love became an entitlement.

From the summer of 1974 until shortly after Jessica was born in June 1975, Helena, Judith and I were cosmopolitan New Yorkers with too little purpose and too much money. Helena and I were not rich—we just behaved as if we were. Judith did not have a dime.

I daily awakened amazed at my good fortune. I was neither confused nor conflicted. Unaware that my relationship with my wife was the romantic ideal of a de-sexed Rotarian, I took for granted that two women could love me and I could love two women. What was so complicated?

More than once, I asked Helena how she would feel if I were to have an affair. She was, after all, my partner. I'd be driving when I asked. The most important conversations in a marriage do not occur in a bed in darkness, but in moving automobiles. As private as bedrooms, steering a vehicle precludes eye contact, a necessary condition to guarantee mutual deception. I posed the question as strictly hypothetical, as close to honesty about my feelings—or lack of them—as I dared to go. Judith and I had not yet done the deed, and for all I knew never would, but I'd be lying to say the thought had not crossed my mind.

Helena said, "I would not want to know about it."

So at a time when the phrase *open marriage* was trendy, a lifestyle being blessed by progressive men and women who understood marriage to be a cage, my spouse opted for ignorance. I had tacit permission to be an adventurer.

I was not stepping out on the sly; my wife and lover knew and liked each other. We were a threesome at movies, rock concerts, restaurants, parks, clubs, parties, shopping expeditions, everywhere but between sheets. None of us was sexually jaded enough to seek that thrill. No questions were asked; no lies were told.

Helena and I had unmoored from the steadier people we'd grown up with: they were accountants or in law school, holding down jobs and becoming citizens. Our expanding social circle was what today we'd call the "creative class." By way of my wealthy sister's expensive decorator, Nat, Helena and I fell in with an uptown circle of mostly gay men, florists, a few dancers, and several itinerant professional ice-skaters. They auditioned for shows and soap operas, and in pre-AIDS, post-Stonewall New York, their lives sparkled. No one *was* anything; everyone planned to *become* something else.

I fit right in. Art teachers plan to become photographers, drama teachers plan to become directors; English teachers—that was me—plan to become novelists.

Helena and I often served as beards for Nat, the pair of straights the decorator needed when entertaining nervous clients. People cracked open their checkbooks when they met the lovely young couple. Nat was smart enough to know he sold himself, not furniture. The decorator might be queer, but he had enough straight friends he could not be so totally flaming a fag that the rumpus room would look like backstage at the *Folies Bergère*. The annual New Year's Eve party at Nat's penthouse close by Central Park was everything you'd expect, right down to the blind piano player and suckling pig. When the Ice Capades hit town, we attended the legendary spaghetti parties.

Judith not only came along, but in that crowd she was the equal to anyone, her repartee and manner level with any of Nat's gay friends, some of the smartest and funniest men I have ever known. Judith was no sidekick. Helena, Judith and I were a set. Everyone in that happy crowd assumed that I slept with both women, either serially or simultaneously. It was probably some lingering hippie-commune-thing that persisted like a post-'60s nasal drip. Why else would the three of us so often show up together?

So I was a Bohemian with a steady job, a social revolutionary collecting a salary, a libertine with a wife who had opted to be blind.

I was drunk enough on my good luck that I imagined we would live openly and happily as a threesome. David Crosby wrote a song, "Triad," that asked *Why can't we go one as three?* Crosby, Stills and Nash sang it, but so did Grace Slick with the Jefferson Airplane. See? Everyone was doing everyone else. But while pop music defines this and all the riffs in this book, having read far too much far too young, my first models were always literary; I knew the arrangement had worked for Percy Shelley, that earliest advocate of Free Love and the liberation of women. Shelley had written that poets were the unacknowledged legislators of the world.

I was simply writing a little legislation.

In our limp times when youth pine in nasal inflections for *relationships* it may be hard to understand that I wanted nothing less than the total, dangerous, obliteration of self in another. I'd have love, to be submerged so totally in another that I would not be drowned, but buoyed up.

Plato speculated that some of us have the misfortune of being animated by half-souls that spend multiple lives searching for the longed for sundered complement. Not all of us. Some of us. Sundered souls endure agony as they drift through mortality longing to commingle spirit and become complete.

Plato made sense to me. Maybe it was no metaphor.

Look, when soul mates find each other, we write songs about it. We carve statues of them. We write plays, poems, epics, legends, ballets and cycles of opera about how the lovers have crossed oceans, pit nations into war, defied the gods, and descended into Death's own Kingdom to reunite.

I am by nature a skeptic, irreligious, doubting, and impatient with anything that claims to be paranormal. Tell me you've seen Grandma Bessie's ghost and you get at best a patronizing smile while I wonder if you are feeble-minded. Talk about astrology, and I will begin my rant on the inadequacies of science education. People who maintain that science and religion simply offer equally valid belief systems are in my opinion engaged in a criminal act that will end the American Experiment.

But when Judith and I came together, I understood why in our hearts all of us need to believe that our corporeal bodies, the mountains, stars, and seas fade away before love is extinguished.

A little grand, I know, but, yeah, being with Judith was like that.

In that mezzanine, Helena and I were 26; Judith was 19. That sounds appallingly now. But if you are expecting some sort of guilt about how the teacher and former student got it on, best skip to the next memoir and leave this riff to be picked over by the Correctness Cops.

I was chronologically ahead of Judith, we were on par spiritually, but she was far ahead of me intellectually and emotionally. We were not about contractual equality. We were not negotiating a *relationship.* She trusted me; I trusted her. There would be no bullshit.

We were in love; falling in love is not an act of will.

For 21st century youth, that idea has about it the whiff of heresy, an aroma as faintly ominous as the ozone that forms around high-tension wires. You are supposed to control your heart in the same way you control calorie intake. My current college students want to believe that matters of the heart are rational, studied decisions. The failure to think life through explains why their parents, that irrational bunch of selfish Boomer fuckups who bought up all the good houses and refuse to die to create job openings, spent so much time in divorce courts.

My current college students will read about romance, usually in connection with a supernatural fantasy, because they are persuaded romance is as real as vampirism. Wholly risk-averse, they avoid commitment while their biological clocks swing past midnight. They hook-up with momentary companions of convenience. Better a quick fuck and cold shower than a far riskier, icky, sure-to-be-a-mess attachment. They delay marriage; they delay children. Their lives are about control managed by delay.

But when Judith and I fell in love, we held hands to leap off a cliff. Weightless in freefall all the way down, we admired the magnificent view of the valley coming faster and faster up at us.

A drama student at NYU, at 163 Judith's IQ was higher than my own. Her beat cynicism was as transparent to me as my faux despair was to her. Judith had been my high school student, of course; how else would I know her IQ? If the odds of meeting your soulmate are a million to one, then there are eight of them in New York City.

Unapologetic intelligence was not an option ordinarily available to 19-year-old girls. Not if they wanted a social life. The callow Brooklyn boys who were Judith's contemporaries could not keep up with her; worse, those louts expected her to feign stupidity. The game left her weary and to some extent certain she would be alone forever.

But here was Glasser, old enough, smart enough, appreciative, over-confident, and just dumb enough not to see oncoming consequences. So what if he had been her teacher?

Love is where you find it.

Three years before we sat in a mezzanine at Radio City Music Hall, a year before she appeared in my senior Honors class, Judith sat alone, cross-legged in jeans on a plot of grass in a park where the high school celebrated Earth Day. While the other girls ran wildly after basketballs, Judith painstakingly strummed her way through the chords of "Casey Jones." I walked up and sang. That made her laugh: the teacher was singing about cocaine. The Dead became "our" band; who else had lyrics about losing poker hands, stacked decks, loaded dice, deals that shouldn't go down, hard luck cowboys, dust, desperadoes, and doom?

We flirted when she became a senior, but the boundaries were clear. We never so much as held hands, exchanged no notes, had no rendezvous. Judith joined my student Chess Club; she joined the Senior Yearbook to which I was adviser. We worked side-by-side long after the official school day ended until past dark when we locked up the high school. It was illegal for me to drive her home, and I never did. I did once take her for a lobster dinner, but that was no date; several other people were along, and we all travelled by taxi. Our ongoing talk was flirtatious, filled with double entendres and movie references. It was edgy fun.

Correctness Cops equate sex and sexuality, a presumption that assumes young women not only lack any psychological or physical resources, but are incapable of forming them. They must be protected from a smile, an act just a few short steps from rape. The only way to protect soon-to-be-victims from predatory men is to outlaw sexuality. The American obsession for safety has transformed men to quivering piles of nervous jelly and encouraged women to run from the shadow of a mirage. In this way, women are safe but infantilized.

With an IQ of 163, Judith was no infant.

Graduation came. I sent Judith a gift—a 45 rpm recording of *Sh-Boom, Life is But a Dream*, by the Chords, a recording already hoary when I found it for her, but a tune I had once been idly humming that she thought was ridiculous, charming, and funny. My address was on the envelope, my telephone number on the card. Subtle, right?

By July, the magic began. I became a wizard.

We met for lunch. Judith chose the Plaza Circle Fountain for that first rendezvous. Our roles had changed. Her former teacher was no longer in charge of what, who, or when. Neither of us had any idea how far this would go. We signed up for a ride and got on-board at the Plaza Circle Fountain on Fifth Avenue, the southeast corner of Central Park, the place where the hansom cabs picked up passengers. *Driver, once around the park.*

I sat on the curling gray marble lip of the fountain, the water spray cool at my back. It was summer. Judith in high-heel sandals came diddy-bopping uptown on Fifth Avenue, a macramé bag bouncing at her shoulder and a huge scarlet begonia fluttering at her ear, homage to the Band Beyond Description, Jehovah's Favorite Choir. Her skirt was homemade by splitting the seams of jeans and restitching them, the skirt covered with more fabric patches than what remained of the original denim. Judith was a hippie born a decade too late. She embroidered a lot of work-shirts with stars, comets and planets, and she worked silver spoons into rings and bangles.

That day, we did nothing more than wander the streets. Near Rockefeller Center we came to a bluegrass band playing "Friend of the Devil," another Dead song. I uninhibitedly sang and dropped $5.00 in a violin case. Maybe that street band's appearance on the sidewalk near St. Patrick's Cathedral was a coincidence, but Judith and I knew the truth of it.

Magic.

A mandolin, banjo and bass playing bluegrass on the streets of Manhattan? Sure, that's likely. And that they play one of our tunes on the first day we meet as what we know we will become lovers? Of course. Of course. Guaranteed. Perfectly logical.

Who could deny such signs and portents? The universe conspired to suit our wishes and needs; if that is not magic, what is?

We agreed to meet again.

The logistics were too easy. Helena did not want to know, so I signed up for chess tournaments. A six round event meant six consecutive Thursdays. In New York City at that time, pay for play chess clubs thrived uptown and downtown, no different from bowling in Sandusky.

All that year, after throwing her arms about my neck whenever we met, we traded gifts, stupid disposable trinkets that Judith always seized with laughter. Even as I write this, standing in a pencil holder on my desk is the cheap black-and-white plastic ballpoint pen she gave me from the St. Jude Shrine in Baltimore. "The patron saint of lost causes," she explained to her Jewish lover.

Our romance played against a soundtrack that transported us far from the canyons of Manhattan. We adored Crosby, Stills and Nash, The New Riders, or

The Jefferson Airplane, those ragged-ass San Francisco bands of tribalism that like the Dead had personnel that promiscuously appeared on each other's recordings, sharing album liner credits for songwriting and anonymously playing backup. Bugger the well-dressed Brits; drown the squeaky clean Beach Boys; Judith and I required three-part harmony sung by people with lots and lots of hair. In a pinch, we settled for the good-old-boy two guitar lead bands like the Allman Brothers or Poco. On a night when Helena simply did not care to come along, we sat on a gymnasium floor at Columbia University to hear The Marshall Tucker Band work through "Fire on the Mountain" and "Take the Highway."

Naked in bed and sated, we practiced her acting class homework. Intoxicated by futility, hopelessness, and our heady sense of star-crossed daring, Judith and I read the dialogue of *Casablanca* to each other. Bogart and Bergman, we would always have Paris.

Though she could credibly hiss Peter Lorre's lines, *Save me, Rick. Save me!* Judith's finest role was as mad Vivien Leigh. She did a persuasive Scarlet O'Hara, but the line of dialogue that most often dropped into our giddier talk was Blanche DuBois's exit in Streetcar; *I have always depended on the kindness of strangers.* Saying it, Judith would collapse with laughter across my chest.

Judith had the knack of being smart and feminine without being foppishly girlish. No games, ever; no worry about how we looked to each other or the world. While she could readily abandon being dainty to sink her canines into a medium-rare hamburger dripping ketchup, she wore tea-rose perfume and was partial to the blocky jewelry she designed and made from silver and copper wire twisted around colored stones and glass beads. The softer skin at her throat always tasted of copper; the valley between her breasts was redolent with flowers.

One afternoon as the winter sun set early and we were in semi-darkness, she lay with me, nearly asleep, and I asked her what in hell she was doing with me. She explained that she had been fucked, did not mind fucking, and lived for those times when she made love. She was sworn to never be fucked again.

And us?

Her head rested on my abdomen, but she looked up through the murky light to see into my eyes. "Something else, Butch. Don't know what to call it. Something else," she said and rolled away from me to hide her face, the only time I'd ever seen her come close to a blush. When she rolled toward me again, her arm went across my throat and she fell asleep, her breath soft on my chest. Thirty minutes later, she jerked awake, amazed. She'd never before fallen asleep in a man's arms.

We found each other mucking around in our thoughts so often that we contemplated the legitimacy of involuntary telepathy, mind-sharing. I once reared up to serve a tennis ball and at the arch of my swing thought of her. No reason, her face flashed into my mind, and so of course I missed the ball completely, swung through, and fell to the ground. My partner thought I was drunk. How do you fall down missing your own serve? When I told Judith of how a stray thought of her had distracted me, she said, "Oh, a woman hates to hear that, Butch."

Many late afternoons, we often met at Brentano's, an upscale bookstore near Washington Square, like so much else, long gone. I once found her on the floor in the poetry aisle with a volume of Keats on her lap. Keats. I was thirty minutes early. Nineteen, Judith passed the time waiting for her lover by reading the doomed tubercular poet who linked death and art.

She'd sat in my classrooms and knew what moved me, of course. She was catching up to me, the English teacher and wannabe writer, but my point is she had the will and ability to catch up. As I sat beside her on the bookstore floor she said, "Listen to this," and because I'd once taught *The Great Gatsby* to her class read the passage for which she'd searched;

Tender is the night,
And haply the Queen-Moon is on her throne,
Cluster'd around by all her starry Fays.

Our afternoons together often ended with an early, light dinner in intimate, neighborhood Greek restaurants. Condensation formed on the front windows. We were surrounded by solicitous and knowing waiters in white shirts, bow ties, and black jackets who poured golden Retsina into wine glasses shining with the refracted flame of a nearby alcohol lamp. Sex wasn't the only reason we were together.

Judith took possession of a room within seconds. She was pretty and she was young, but it was more than that. She had presence. She only gradually was growing aware of her power, new to a 19-year-old. It startled her, though never so much that she did not fail to bat her eyes to obtain the best table, the best service, the suggestion of a fine wine, and the complimentary dessert. Of course we would be back; what restaurant would not want two such young lovers to return? We must have been very pretty to look at.

Judith was short, olive-skinned and under her coat was capable of wearing nothing above her waist except a man's white tuxedo vest, one she found in a consignment shop. Bras were outré. Young and bold, she had a figure like an erotic Hindu carving, but being Italian she had a face she herself described as "the map of Sicily." Her eyes were perfectly black streaked with hazel, and I don't need to tell you the rest.

Shortly after Jessica was born, Judith ended our affair. Helena's pregnancy was confirmed by a phone call from a physician to Nat's place. All three members of the triad were there. Nat giggled at the news, and he opened a better wine so we could celebrate, Helena's last drink for seven months. She also gave up cigarettes.

Never out to steal me away, only to steal some time, once my child was in the world, Judith chose to no longer ignore consequences. Helena might opt to be blind, but Judith would not. A new soul complicated the soul-mate equation, and since I could never have summoned the courage to say we were done, the job was hers.

So Judith became Bogart. I became Bergman. It was time for me to stop talking nonsense and get on that plane.

Life took me to the Arizona desert. When John Lennon was shot, Judith called me, weeping. By that time, Helena had long known all the facts. She believed she had forgiven me. Maybe she had in her head, but if this memoir is about anything it is about how the heart is not subject to deliberate control.

While I took Judith's call, Helena sat in the kitchen staring through me. Remember, Judith had been her friend, too.

A year or so later, before I headed to Iowa and my first college teaching gig, Judith married, and then, for a variety of reasons for which my time with Judith was only a small part, Helena and I divorced.

It was six years after the rendezvous at the Plaza Fountain.

I looked Judith up during one of my swings through the East.

It was the more perilous '80s. We met in a Greenwich Village diner and ordered grilled cheddar cheese sandwiches and dark beer. Judith was anxious, impatient to be gone, having agreed to join me only to settle a debt. In prior years, she'd contacted me a several times when things were not so hot for her, so in the equations that are the basis of the algebra of the heart, she owed me. She'd called when there had been problems with her husband, and when a car accident spared her life, she was certain that in some mystical way I had to be reassured she was all right and must have known what happened.

She still took the magic for granted.

Her hair was dyed a perfect shiny metallic black, and she'd cut it so short it seemed a helmet. She wore a blue business suit, pumps and a frilly crimson tie. Sugar Magnolia was no more. Her eyes shone with the steely unforgiving glint of cocaine, a hit plainly taken to get her through this evil, torturous, dangerous, foul, poisonous lunch. Her fingers drummed the table, the painted nails far too long to play a guitar. Beneath the table, her knee quivered anxiously. She kept looking over her shoulder. *C'mon Butch, give it up. Fold the hand; it was time to quit.*

We spent an awful hour in a drafty diner over those sandwiches, a far cry from grape leaves, olives and feta. Not a glass of Retsina was in sight.

She said, "Look, Butch, you want to carry me in your head as some eternal ideal. That's you, but that's not me. I won't be some symbol for you." She said it as if angry. She echoed Bogart in *The Maltese Falcon*—*I won't play the sap for you*. She wanted me to release her. She'd dismissed me years ago, carried on, and here I was again, the bad penny returned.

As I said, she was smarter than I. My last emotional chip lost, her heart's debt paid, I pushed away from the game, busted.

I am here to report that romantic love is out there, hot, passionate, unannounced, life-altering, intoxicating and magical. I hear you say, "Oh cut the shit, Glasser. You followed your dick and you cannot write your way around that." You'll want to say that Glasser rationalizes bad behavior. Go ahead. Shake your finger in my face. You'll want to say that Glasser is dumb enough to believe a hormonal rush is love divine. You may even want to howl for the blood of the teacher who took up with a high school student mere weeks after she graduated.

Whatever you think, I cannot deny recounting to you the episode without abandoning total honesty. I must be some kind of sap. But I just report.

You can think all that. I can't stop you. But you'd be wrong.

Physicists do mind experiments to find the truth of things that cannot be measured in real time and space. Surely, we can do the same for the heart.

So let us suppose Plato had it right. Suppose two souls sundered could spend mortal lives in perpetual search for their counterparts. Suppose I'd left Helena at the worst possible time, pregnant, in order to connect with Judith at the best possible time. We'd have uncrossed the stars that were star-crossed. Suppose for just this once I'd not delayed my own happiness, that impulse that was to become a theme of my life, forever choosing to be the responsible *mensche* delaying his personal gratification. Suppose that one time I leaned far off center and risked falling to snatch at the one shining brass carousel ring among the tens of thousands bent from plain iron. Suppose Tristran and Isolde. Suppose Dante and Beatrice. Suppose Heathcliff and Catherine. Suppose Paola and Francesca. Suppose all that.

Hypothesize earthly bliss, yet you know the next questions as well as I do.

What then? Would I be who I am now? Would my daughter? Would Judith? Her children? What worlds would have been traded away? What maintained? All those roads not taken lead only to more roads in an infinite number of universes dreamed but never realized.

So I will not guess at what never was and never could be, but now celebrate the truth of a moment when the earth vanished beneath my feet and I soared free of time and space.

I report: Love exists.

I know this to be true because in late 1974, in the darkened mezzanine of Radio City Music Hall, I sat between my wife and my lover. Bonnie Raitt on the stage below sat on a simple three-legged stool. In the shadows beyond the puddle of her spotlight, a guy named Freebo accompanied her on a Fender Fretless bass. Bonnie Raitt sang:

I've had bad dreams too many times
To think that they don't mean much anymore
Fine times have gone and left my sad home
And the friends who once cared just walk out my door.

But love has no pride when I call out your name
And love has no pride when there's no one to blame.

Thunder Road
Bruce Springsteen

Brenda had no illusions about who I was or what she was about. I'd never heard the phrase, *transition woman* until she used it. "You're in the PDFF," she said. "That makes you fair game." The campus health bar was mobbed with people carrying plastic trays and healthy lunches. I asked; she explained, "Post-Divorce Fucking Frenzy," and wiped an orange mustache of carrot juice from her lip.

I was her college teacher and she was a freshman in my Honors class, an assignment that was a gift to me from the program director for three years of good work during my graduate writing student career. I had an assistantship: I taught Composition, they paid me pennies; I attended my classes for free.

The assignment was a gift because those twenty-five kids had been selected from an entering class of 2,500: they were brilliant, and Brenda was among the best of the best. With beauty, wealth, intelligence, and an irrepressible sense of adventure, she showed me how life could once again be possible.

Her sole liability was certain death at an early age.

Two years before Brenda ordered her carrot juice, I was sure my life that had been teetering on the brink in the east had in the west been pulled back from disaster. Helena had forgiven my transgression—at least she said as much. We owned two Tucson condos, living in one, renting the other. The sun always shone. Except for the fact there was no ocean, everyone on campus looked as well-toned as extras from a Hollywood surfer movie. I played a lot of tennis, taught a little, and became trim running in the hills where we lived at the west edge of town. In the shade of our backyard patio, hammering away on my Smith-Corona 220 for so many hours our neighbors assumed I was handicapped and eked out a living addressing envelopes, I'd written a terrible novel about a sensitive public school teacher who falls in love with a student.

We lived close enough to the university that I traveled by bicycle, a big, absurd pink plastic kid-seat mounted on the rear wheel, where Jessica, 5, sat and shouted "Faster!" when I stood on the pedals straining to crest hills. On the downhill run to her daycare center, we coasted by a horse ranch. The air was rich with the smell of manure and piss, and Jessica laughed at the wind and our speed as I shouted to the arid landscape, "Does it get any better than this?"

But one awful night, my wife and I were making love when it felt to me as if Helena was not there. I asked her what was going on. She cried. While I'd been inhaling horse piss and pursuing my dreams, she'd found what she needed.

I'd been in love; now it was her turn.

Divorce in Arizona was easier than buying tacos. For Jessica's sake, we took our shot at counseling. Summing up a session, our counselor mixed a metaphor more accurate than any possible cliché. She said, *Maybe too much water has flowed under the dam.*

Never mind that my life was crumbling, I chose to be scandalized at the lack of her language skills. I needed to be indignant. What kind of idiot had we hired to help us? Water flows *under* bridges or *over* dams. I fumed over this until I realized the phrase was apt if the dam or bridge has collapsed into rubble.

Helena chose not to show up at the divorce proceeding. The judge assumed her whereabouts were unknown, when in fact Helena was nearby across town shaping her new life from the wreckage of her old. These proceedings had nothing to do with who she was going to be. After fifteen minutes of close questioning, a twelve year marriage dissolved as neatly as any failed business arrangement might. Joint custody of Jessica, and a negotiated fifty-fifty on property. No alimony. No child support. Done and done. Slam the gavel. "See the clerk." Hail and farewell. *Mazel* and *baruch*.

Helena was free to discover new ways to defy her parents' expectations.

In a space of four months, Helena moved out, told her boss to fuck himself, was fired, met another man, became pregnant, remarried, found another job, and suffered a miscarriage. The Polish-Jewish girl who'd majored in Russian literature and played ruthless Bridge and Poker, a woman who in New York had worked years as a high level state civil servant while earning postgraduate degrees at night in business and counseling, a woman who'd been amused by our New York gay friends who swore by their personal astrologer, that same woman suddenly deemed her most prized possessions to be the rocks in her pockets, crystals whose auras she relied upon to keep her well and happy. With the awe and conviction of a new convert, she explained to me how channeling had brought her into contact with her larger soul; in dreams, she saw her own death in dozens of former lives, always of a lung disease. An alcoholic and rehab counselor, she'd fallen for a guy in her own drunk tank. He was ten years her junior, tattooed, subscribed to *Easy Rider Motorcycle Magazine*, and had barely finished high school before giving his life over to cheap wine and the long and winding road.

Helena had forever loved Dean Moriarty. Now she had found him in the flesh. In the desert, with a .45 Browning, for sport they blasted silhouette targets into shreds.

I had no idea what I might do. To return to New York City to revive my high school teaching license seemed the act of a beaten man. *Put your boyish dreams away, Glasser. Nice try on that piece-of-shit novel, but you're a civil servant whose dreams of artistic glory rest on a narcissistic imagination that confuses bold adventure with sordid self-indulgence. Go back, hang on thirty-five years, never think a thought, and a generous pension shall be granted unto you forever and forever world without end. Amen.*

The future was empty. My past was a cold ruin. On the one hand, that felt like crap, but on the other, if I could look forward, it felt like a universe of opportunity was opening. Mistakes could not matter. Everything I could lose was already lost.

In that health bar, my student Brenda explained to me, "The odds are fifty-fifty I'll be dead at 32." She said this as if she were reporting the average rainfall in Mozambique. She was 18. Her interest in me was no pose; it was Brenda's conscious goal to pack as much experience as possible into the little time she had.

She lived fast and expected to die young, but because of juvenile diabetes she had no illusions about leaving a pretty corpse. If they did not hack off her limbs, it would be her eyes; if not her eyes, it would be her kidneys. She'd chosen me to be her older man. Her French nurse had shared with her that every young woman needed an older man, and she could not very well wait until she was old herself, say 25, as that might not happen at all. She simply had no time for boys. Besides, they bored her. She hoped I would not mind.

I'd slept with a former student, but Brenda made her way to my bed while still in my class.

It's going to be hard not to squirm at this one if your membership badge in the Correctness Cops is still shiny. I was getting no younger and evidently no wiser. Worse yet, Brenda was right: I was in the PDFF. I am fully aware that student-teacher affairs can be a mess, but I needed a behavior that if I survived would validate me as male and allow me to feel in control and sexually attractive.

I never pursued Brenda. She came at me.

While some will snort I should have run harder

and faster, bear in mind there could be no question of abuse of power. I was no pest, leering daily at a young woman who had no choice but to appear in my classroom to be subjected to yet more leers. Nor could I extort Brenda—no one in that Honors class would earn any grade but an A. As for my exploiting her emotional maturity, with her heightened sense of imminent mortality, she had me cold. By her standards, she was in her twilight years.

Brenda's hometown, Camelback Mountain in Scottsdale, is one of the richest ZIP codes in America. The French maid who raised Brenda and her three sisters was known as *Nana*, of course. Brenda at 18 could savor Coquilles St. Jacques, sip a Chardonnay and simultaneously gush over Nana's scrumdilicious sugar-free desserts and the drop-dead cute stuffed animal she'd seen in Goldwater's. Brenda occupied the townhouse condo Daddy bought on the certainty that at least two of his kids would live there while they attended the state university, so he took tax deductions where most people pay dorm fees, and eventually he sold at a profit.

In addition to economic advantages, Brenda was physically breathtaking. She confessed to 5 feet 11 inches, but she was obviously taller. She disliked team sports and refused to play basketball or volleyball, leaving high school coaches distraught. She simply had no time for such crap. She habitually wore a white T-shirt and blue jeans cut to her hips, the fringe of loose threads floating around her thighs, a flat-chested Daisy Mae striding barefoot from the Sonora Desert. She wore no jewelry, she wore no belt, her shirt had no logo, message or print. Her skin was butter-colored. Often shoeless, she strode into class as though it was her living room or an extension of the desert she so loved. Her hair was parted in the center, so nearly white it seems improper to call it blonde, long enough to whirl about her arms, straight and thick over her shoulders and back. When she'd been 15, her face had adorned the cover of the Girl Scouts Calendar. At 16, they demoted her to November.

She seemed assembled of incorrectly matched parts—the long lines from hip to knee and from knee to ankle were disproportionate to the line from hip to chin—so she should have appeared awkward, ungainly, likely to topple. Tall women frequently slouch; Brenda walked like a super-model, a career she'd considered until she realized it meant living indoors and never eating well. My Girl-Scout-lover took me camping north of Payson in the pine forests on the Mogollon Rim, the high country of northern Arizona, far beyond civilization. We hiked for hours from her car, an uphill trek under a backpack that damn near killed me. Her flat-footed walk cast before her an incredible distance one of those legs until her foot found the ground, her weight shifted as though her pelvis were a gymbal, and she boomed forward. Her arms swung with it. She rarely wore a bra; no need. Proud, shoulders back, she moved with neither arrogance nor apology. It was all I could do to keep up with her. We spent two nights and two days on a mountainside, and during that time while rain unceasingly pelted the tent when I saw her administer an insulin injection, she explained her likely future of blindness, kidney failure, amputation and premature death.

Brenda traveled regularly with an Arab prince. His father, the sheik, sent him to the University of Arizona to study desert agriculture. His smarter, oldest brother studied petroleum engineering at Stanford. Brenda's sort-of-boyfriend supplied the prince with drugs and companions. "It's just for show," Brenda said and her big hand closed around five or six green grapes she glommed at a gulp. I believed her.

The boyfriend was in thrall to the prince's blue Ferrari, a vehicle in which Brenda did not look half-bad when the top was down. Brenda also looked pretty good climbing the gangway of the prince's Lear jet. They snow-skied in Aspen on Saturday; water-skied in San Diego on Sunday; at Brenda's insistence returned to Tucson and Freshman English by Monday promptly at 10 o'clock. She never missed class.

Brenda anticipated becoming a research physician with every intention of curing her own disease. These are not the priorities of a part-time call-girl; if the boyfriend and the prince schemed for anything more than a showpiece, they burned a lot of jet fuel without coming to know Brenda as I was to. Once a girl scout, always a girl scout.

I was 34 and wholly amazed that this statuesque beauty with ash white hair, blue eyes and a 38-inch inseam, a jet-setter in the true sense of that tiresome phrase, believed she needed a fling with a man fresh off a failed marriage who not only drove a yellow Chevette that needed a muffler and had a twisted coat hanger jammed into the broken socket as a radio antenna, but as his other vehicle did not fly a jet but pedaled a rusted bicycle to deliver his daughter to the Three Bears Day School. Why fly to Aspen when Glasser is right here at home? The first time she pushed my Chevette's seat back as far as it could go to accommodate her legs, she told me that the Ferrari had a three-spigot bar built into the dash—vodka, gin and scotch. She was pretty sure the veneer was real wood, not plastic, but if I wanted she would check on that important detail.

I know people who'd take Brenda's deal in a New-York-minute. Hell, I know people who would accept the deal for a ride in that Ferrari, leave alone the Lear jet, or the weekends skiing in Vail or Telluride. Brenda's acceptance of doom left me slack-jawed with wonder. It put my petty troubles in perspective. By the time Brenda would be my age, she expected to be in the ground. My divorce was not the end of anything, and I was stupid for thinking so.

The day we became an item, I was babbling about mammals and fur. Teachers get into the damndest discussions, and vanity had me looking into transplants for my receding hairline. Why, I asked, did eyebrow hair grow to a certain length and quit, but the follicles on our heads sprouted hair even after we were dead? How did body hair plugged into a bald man's head learn to grow again? Ordinarily, when I go off like that, a class will cover their grins and take it as certain evidence that their teacher is slightly dotty, but two hours after class Brenda showed up in my shared office with an explanatory article she'd razored out of an obscure science journal. I did not understand a word of it. She explained the biology and organic chemistry required. We enjoyed the role reversal—she became the teacher. We talked. The talk ran into dinner. That proved so nice, we went again. It was like that.

All this is to tell you that I completely fell forever in love with Brenda the specific morning after the first night we slept together. This is the reverse of the preferred order, true enough. We'd dined at Scordato's, an Italian restaurant in the western foothills where we sat on a tiled patio overlooking the city. Without recourse to the menu, I'd ordered *Corvo Blanco,* a label I knew as a New Yorker, a gesture that made her laugh when the waiter's eyes glowed approval. Brenda, I later learned, often timed her insulin to maximize the effect of wine. We skipped dessert to get to my place. I paid the babysitter. It was my first time in years with a woman not my wife. I have no memory of the sex.

In the morning, my daughter, Jessica, came into the bedroom. Eager to escape to her new life, Helena had left our daughter with me. Jessica's six-year-old eyes clouded puzzlement at the sight of the very tall naked lady in bed with Daddy. Brenda lifted the corner of the blanket and patted the place between us. "Come on in," she said, which Jessica did and immediately fell asleep. Mind you, this gesture that saved my daughter's psychological life and made my future as a single parent possible was delivered by a woman who was all of 18. Sure, she was gorgeous, smart, rich and sophisticated, but this was a different order of things, as different as a blue Ferrari is from a yellow Chevette. She could have giggled. She could have stammered. Who'd have blamed her if she'd clutched the sheet to her chest and beaten a hasty retreat to the bathroom? But no—she not only let my kid think Daddy and she were engaged in perfectly acceptable grown-up behavior, but that the behavior did not encroach upon or threaten Jessica's relationship with me. I bless Brenda still.

That afternoon I fastened a hook-and-eye lock into the door molding. Seventy-nine cents worth of discretion from a hardware store is a can't-beat-it bargain.

We spent a few weekends on Mexican beaches. Driving my car at 100 miles per hour through the Organ Pipe Monument, a cactus forest, one bare leg draped out the window as she steered with her other knee, with two hands she twisted the key to open a tin of pâté. Her favorite white wine was *Vouvray*, and she kept it chilled in a metal Army-issue thermos. It was my honor and duty to hand her the thermos when she asked for it, which she did after smearing huge gobs of the pâté from her Swiss Army knife onto French soda crackers. She did not use the thermos' cup, but drank from it directly. Each time she swallowed more wine, we sped a little faster and her toes wiggled a bit more in the hot, dry wind rushing over the Chevette's side-view mirror. Since my car's radio was unacceptably unreliable and there was no English music station in Mexico, she'd thrown a portable boom-box into the shallow back seat. The thing played *Thunder Road* again and again, so loud that the desiccated Mexican cows took notice. Each time the band got to the saxophone solo, she'd shout encouragement, "Blow Clarence, blow!" and on the line, *Show a little faith, there's magic in the night*, she leaned across the narrow car and kissed me with winey lips. I don't doubt that Clarence Clemmons, the Big Man, heard her shout his name. I learned to have a little faith.

How it is we did not roll the car is a mystery. The Chevette bounded across the land, raising a plume of dust that could be seen in Chicago, or at least in St. Louis. When we crossed the border on *Via Ocho*, we pushed on to *Puerto Penasco*, Rocky Point, a fishing village on the Gulf of California.

Puerto Penasco has since been given over to developers and high-rise beachfront condos, but back then, to avoid dysentery, we had to port our own water from the US. In the town, all we could trust to eat were bread, milk, cheese and shrimp. In the early morning after we watched the seals waddle back into the sea, we left the beach and walked uphill on a treacherously sharp sidewalk made of concrete and broken seashells. At the bakery, the rolls were so hot they were painful to hold. When we broke the rolls, they emitted steam and we burned our fingers. The woman at the bakery sliced very yellow butter off a soft block and it quickly melted on the steaming bread where she placed it. "*Lechè*," she said, and, as if we were children who knew nothing, gestured toward a cooler. The milk was heavy and rich with unhomogenized cream, and while we sat on the bakery's stone steps, we gulped it from cool glass bottles and licked the butter from our fingers while the sun climbed the hazy sky and warmed us. Brenda and I ran on the crescent beach and swam in the sea. In the evenings, we cooked the shrimp sold live on the dock and drank beer. In Mexico, there is never a shortage of beer. The beer was so cold, the bottles contained slivers of ice. We grilled the shrimp in garlic and butter on a fire we built on the beach. We listened to the surf and watched the moon float above the Gulf of California. We slept in a tent on the sand. In the morning, we awoke to the barking seals and the day began again.

In my final spring in Tucson, the air was redolent with jacaranda and orange blossoms. Brenda taught me to run in the *arroyos* of the desert. She ritualized stretching, bending, leaning into it. Jogging with her, I had to take three steps to every two of hers. I was a dwarf in a footrace with a Valkyrie.

One time we ran two or three miles through the desert on the eastern edge of town near her condo. Back in her air-conditioned living room, we sprawled onto her blue shag carpet. We were sweaty. We were giddy. We were in love. One thing led to another. Brenda developed two oval burns marks on her back. Friction with the shag rug left my knees raw.

Two days later, I flew to Des Moines to interview for a job at Drake University. Before the jet departed Tucson, I had time to meet my Honors class in the morning. I was trim, fit, tan, wearing khaki chinos and a blue poplin blazer, my interview outfit, and I was holding forth at the front of the room on some idiocy when one of the women in the class pointed at my knees. Blood like stigmata oozed through the cloth. My students all knew I was bound for an interview. There was no time to change into a fresh outfit. "Club soda." "Cold water." "No, warm water, but blot, don't smear." They were helpful.

I said something about stumbling while running through the desert and looked up. At the back of the room where she always sat because of her height, Brenda had one long, bare, awe-inspiring leg resting at the ankle on an empty chair before her. Her pencil played near the corner of her lip. Her skintight pink cotton top was sleeveless.

She theatrically winced and touched her back. She ached from her own wounds.

No words can describe her wicked, wicked smile, nor are there words to describe how later as my jet lifted off I marveled again at her. If Brenda's certain knowledge of mortality could grace her with such presence and could not rob her of the ability to love, then the dark unknown life to which I was going far from family and friends was one I could enter without fear.

I got the job.

L.A. Woman
The Doors

Decorah is in northeast Iowa. Luther College is there. I don't know what else might be. I suspect not much.

They invite me to do a reading. My first book of short fiction has won a prize. I've thought of myself as a writer for a long time, but being certified has a whole new feel.

The place is two hours from the nearest interstate. To this New York City boy transplanted to Iowa, that fact alone seems exotic. No one passes through Decorah. No one travels to Decorah. Decorah is neither a destination nor a stopover. Why the hell is Decorah there? Gee, already I am learning how being a real writer can take a real person to real places…and, all right, Decorah isn't Stockholm, but I'd drive several nights and days for a smidgen of recognition.

To impress the hoi-polloi with my great heart, I plan to read a powerful story of gritty realism, but when this woman built like a semi with crosses on her uniform's dark lapels stands, everyone in the dining hall joins hands and she leads us in Grace. I am a nice Jewish boy, one not likely to be smitten with Holy Revelation, but I see the error of my ways. This, Glasser, is *Luther* College, get it? A profane tale of desire read by the Brooklyn-born Yid who snatched the maraschino cherry from the top of his fruit salad before prayer will not be well received. I stop flirting with the undergrads, all of whom seem to be corn-silk blonde girls fed on buttermilk, and I mentally opt for a more sedate tale, one that will prevent a pogrom.

I am at last a writer, young, male, old enough to seem worldly, young enough that when I am introduced there is a titter and giggle that I know has nothing to do with the high-mindedness of the occasion, nothing less than the Cause of Literachure and Belly Letters.

After my reading, there is no drinking, no party. Never mind a bacchanal, by ten o'clock the brownie plate holds only crumbs and the OJ container is sticky and empty. Gripping a lectern, I answer the magic questions: I write in the morning. Yes, I use a pencil and big yellow pads. No, I can't speak for other writers. The kids are earnest. These questions need to be asked. I smile and nod. This earnest school in an earnest corner of earnest Iowa is paying me one hundred dollars to be earnest. At the evening's end, my host, an earnest guy with a thin neck, a scraggly beard, and a rash on his earnest Adam's apple, leads me to a dormitory room so earnest the cinder block walls have been painted beige. There is a chair, a desk, a lamp, and a mattress curled back on itself on the bed frame. As he straightens the mattress and withdraws a pillowcase from the desk, my host talks about what he calls "my art and our struggle." I respond and do not laugh. He's earnest, and who am I with my one book in print to think him anything but a peer?

At 1:00 a.m., comes a soft knock at the door.

This perquisite of being the writer is maybe 20. She is dark-haired, long shining tresses that loop below her waist, jeans, a gray sweatshirt with a torn collar showing a very white bra strap on a very fair shoulder, no shoes, no socks. Her eyes are downcast as she tells me she wants to write. That's all. Just write. Her room is on the floor above mine. She carries a lighted votive candle in a water glass. She could not sleep. I tell her I understand; I too was sleepless. We share something, sleeplessness. She is plain, round-faced, and I realize I could drown in her chocolate eyes, but she has about her that air of desperation I have already marked in so many women from the Midwest, that tension at the base of her throat like the pulse of a panicked rabbit, an unarticulated resignation to the sure knowledge that she will live and die in these vast open spaces among men who equate strength with silence.

And here am I, the writer. A voice.

We talk and smoke together; a touch of human communion is what she most requires, and the candlelight and overflowing ashtray offer a taint of mundane danger, as well. After an hour, I beg fatigue and I usher her out, unkissed. Will she lie to her friends? Do they know she was here? I might have been her first.

In my late night dream, she is grown to a lush, cornfed beauty, wanton and eager, innocent and willing. In my dream, her breath smells sweet as hay, her breasts hard and full. I could have done anything, anything at all. Once, I awaken and ask myself, *Why not, why not?*

Morning, I throw my book bag into my car. I am to

teach a class back in Des Moines at 11:00. Before me stretches a four-hour drive from the edge of nowhere, where I am, to central nowhere, where I need to be.

After years of humping the rusted 4-cylinder Chevette through America, with a steady job I treated myself to a muscle car, a throwback to my sports car and motorcycle days. My newly purchased standard-shift Camaro eases me into the landscape. I'd arrived in early winter darkness and so had not seen the land surrounding Decorah, but now in the February dawn I take in the rolling hills, winter's brown earth, white silos, still cows in frozen fields, and that limitless flat Iowa horizon beneath a rising, heatless, colorless sun. Light ignites hoarfrost with cold flame.

The scene is breathtaking. Atop a small rise, I have to stop simply so I can see and remember. I want this moment forever. I step from the vehicle and walk once around the car. Has air ever felt this sharp, this crisp, or this new? This landscape is so obvious and so sentimental that if I were not in it I would mock any report of it, but leaning against my car's warm hood in this February Iowa morning, my arms crossed at my chest, I am solemn. The cold air barely stirs. The trees are black fingers. Only the cows slowly move.

So this is what is in Decorah. This is what the girl who wants to write wants to escape. I am her emissary from elsewhere, but how can she not know what she already has?

There is no more time to lose. As I snap the car into second gear, my car radio finds a station from Iowa City, a college town, maybe the best college town in

America. Before I find third, squeezed from the dashboard speaker comes Jim Morrison. Jim shrieks and moans about the L.A. woman.

> *Are you a lucky little lady in The City of Light*
> *Or just another lost angel?*

In this landscape, who could put together what they see with what I hear? Nothing will merge. The universe lifts its skirts before our eyes, but we are clueless as to what, what, what it means. The girl and I know this. We will be writers. We know this. You are a writer. You know this. You know how it happens. First there is *this*. Then there is *that*. You make connections. You draw lines. A coherent new picture emerges. But to impose sense on it is finally only an illusion of will. I'll be a better writer. I'll struggle to draw the lines yet another way, and what was incoherent will become something else. I know that *Mr. Mojo Risin'* is an anagram of *Jim Morrison*. I know that. Everyone should know that. But what is that knowledge beside this landscape of fire, ice, art, prayer, innocence and longing under a heatless sun? The elements won't come together. The mole on the belly of this exquisite whore might be the maraschino cherry on my unblessed cup of fruit. Last night's easy taste of virtue is already below the horizon behind me, and this morning I awake speeding through countryside in the grip of cold flame, nothing before me but Jim Morrison's high-octane ode to restlessness. Joining hands to pray. My art, our struggle. The girl. That sweet, sweet girl. Me, here, now. It won't work together. None of it will work.

I accelerate. The volume cranks. Oh, yes, this too is me.

L.A womaaaaaan, you're my womaaaaaaan.

I soar over the road at 80, 90, 100 miles per hour, a road slick with black ice. It's dawn. The Camaro and I slice through a Currier and Ives print. My muscle car violates a frozen cornfield while behind me I've left a country girl untouched. My passenger compartment holds me, the writer, in my womb of private urban madness, while in the white farmhouses that dot the land families eat golden pancakes and hot brown biscuits running with yellow butter. They drink scalding sweet dark coffee made in great blue speckled iron pots. They down whole meals of virtue every day.

City of night. City of night. City of night!

At 120 miles per hour, the car vaults over a bump. For a heartbeat, I am aloft. My empty stomach rises to my chin before it drops to my balls when the car hits the ground. But I am singing. No, I am howling, howling louder than Jim, my palms slapping the wheel. The sun is not a half hand over the horizon at the start of this new day, but me and Jim are in the City of Night in God's own northeast corner of Iowa.

Jim was already long dead, but I sure am not. Not me, Jim-bo. My hands tingle at the wheel's cold. I blow into my fist. I don't need to know what any of it means. It is enough to be in it.

I am inside; I am outside, I am everywhere.

Sweet Dreams of You
Patsy Cline

When I met the video store girl, I was sleeping with women because I knew I could. Or to find out if I could. It amounts to the same thing.

I'd open my eyes in the morning and before my feet touched a cold floor I'd wonder if that night I would be with someone that I had not yet met.

Sex is affirmation. It was necessary to feel desirable. It was necessary to feel male. If that makes me predatory, let the Correctness Cops grind their teeth. I can live with it.

I looked good; I felt good; I harmed no one; I lied to no one; I did not persist where I was unwelcome. In Iowa, polite deferred gratification, that most middle class virtue, washed from me like water in a shower. Responsible to no one but myself, I taught my college classes, wrote four or so hours each day, lifted light weights, played a bit of tennis, stretched, crunched 50 sit-ups, and on some days ran as many as five miles. I missed Jessica, but otherwise I was happy.

Came summer, with my first semesters as a professor behind me, the long Iowa days became ever longer. Alone, in the humid evening as the sun set, with my ass on one of the three hard cool cement steps that led into my house, I smoked until I saw only the ember of my cigarette and the colder light of fireflies. Then I went inside and watched movies on a tiny Panasonic desktop color TV with an eight-inch screen—all I could tolerate. I hated television. I'd bought it for Jessica's first visit to Iowa that first winter recess, but we never so much as plugged it in. After that, I rented a video player so I could see Big Movies on my tiny screen. To watch the damned thing, it had to be lifted from the floor where I stowed it beneath the kitchen table.

The video rental place was a shack in the parking lot of a strip mall in a western suburb of Des Moines. Des Moines has suburbs for the same reason it has a symphony orchestra, as a pretense toward sophistication. To a New York City boy, downtown Des Moines seemed to be located a convenient spitting distance from out of town Des Moines. I'd spent three months driving home hearing on the radio about heavy rush hour traffic until I was oriented enough to realize I was in the thick of it.

The girl behind the video store counter had that vacant stare the girls who folded shirts at the laundromat develop—here, but elsewhere, all at once. One side of the store was for Beta tapes, the other for VHS. The business was new. The same guys who made fortunes emptying quarters from washers and dryers saw in video stores a way to make a pile with a small outlay of cash, and so they fished in the same labor pool for women either dumb enough to be honest or with imagination so limited that they stole only tolerable amounts.

The video clerk's dark hair was long and lustrous. In

New York, Judith's hair had been like that. She'd clutch a gathered sheet to her throat with one hand after we made love, and from behind her, I'd watch her before an oval mirror while she brushed that hair. The movements were deliberate, smooth and practiced. From my angle, the flare of her hips, her bare back bent to the side, the tug of her brush as she ran it up and out from underneath her hair—it was pure grace. From time to time, she would turn and take my cigarette, inhale once deeply, and hand the cigarette back to me in our communion of sin.

In Des Moines, that memory was a comfort. Like most men, I am always prepared to make an ass out of myself trying to replicate the past, so when the video girl's hair beckoned from my imperfect romanticized memory, I should have had the sense to know this was not a good thing. But loneliness stifles good sense.

I ask the video girl what time she is off from work.

She goes, What do you do?

I tell her. She does not believe me. A college professor. Sure. I read doubt in her eyes. Professors were always walking into her life and asking for a date. Just last week she had to break it off with a physicist. So she goes, did I plan to take her some place? Any place, I say. Name it. She says ten o'clock.

Ten o'clock. From my car, I watch her lock up. I'd parked, smoked, a father and professor with artistic ambitions deluding himself into thinking he was still dangerous. The video clerk is a little surprised that I return for her, and she is uncomplicated enough to be flattered by that. She refuses one of my cigarettes, fiddles with my car's radio tuner, and says she likes The Yellow Rose.

If there is a town in the Midwest or Southwest or Northwest that does not have a roadhouse named The Yellow Rose, I have not heard of it. Gravel in the parking lot. Set back from the road in a cinderblock structure half in the woods. Clouds of moths thick as Biblical plagues swirl up cones of white lights. Pickups parked helter-skelter from the edge of the two-lane blacktop to the murky shadow where damp woods begin. Pool tables, thick smoke, dim lights, and loud, loud music played by musicians behind chicken wire, their only protection from thrown beer bottles. They got wet, but no skull fractures.

We are a ways from suburban Des Moines. We are a ways from suburban anywhere. This is the place where drunken good ol' boys do homicide with bare hands for the honor of Betty Lou, a place where the weapon of choice is "a shod foot," the legalism that means someone kicked the teeth and living snot out of someone else.

Into The Yellow Rose we go, and with God as my witness the cover band has a singer who is doing a creditable imitation of Patsy Cline crooning "Sweet Dreams of You." You can have Rolling Rock, Coors draft or Bud; that's the limit of beverage service. I shell peanuts and the video girl tells me she is 26. I tell her she looks younger, which is true. Still, her job, that time, that place, she is a "girl." Her voice is raw, a shouted whisper. Maybe she'd gargled battery acid. Was I really a professor at the university? I am much too young to be a professor. I say I am and show her my ID card and she shakes her head as though she will allow a little harmless fiction backed by an elegant forgery. Maybe a fake professor ID gets me privileges at the library. She herself has two semesters at community college. She hopes someday for a job as a bank teller. Before a second beer, she wants it understood that I am not getting into her pants. She makes that crystal clear. No way.

We eat Goldfish and peanuts by the handful while she tells me she despises pinball and is not about to watch me shoot 8-Ball with the farmers and sons of farmers who throw back shots of JD and Wild Turkey from pint bottles they carry in brown paper bags. But she is willing to dance, which we do.

She shows me the Two-Step. I can endure any amount of humiliation on a dance floor if it means dancing with anyone with hair like that who can fill a pair of jeans so neatly. I take her hand. It is oddly rough, far beyond callused, hard and smooth as the cold green glass bottle that held her beer. I go, what kind of work did you do to make your hands like that?

People will tell a stranger anything. I've never been shy.

But the video girl does not care to share the story of her hand. She goes, not tonight. We down two more and she says she has to leave. I drive back to the strip mall and her car. Before she leaves me, we squeeze each other beerily, nothing more than any two junior high kids might do if they had a moon as fat and hazy as that one, and as soon as my lips approach her ear or throat she pushes me away so there is no mistake about who is in control. But pushing me away, I feel her right hand. Coarse as her left.

That week, I rent *Star Wars*, *Five Easy Pieces*, and *2001: A Space Odyssey*, odd movies for an eight-inch screen, to be sure, but renting movies takes me to the video store. The video girl sees no point to my attention. If I am who I say I am, there is no future to this, and if I am a lying son-of-a-bitch with a fake ID, why would she want to be with a lying son-of-a-bitch? But I say I like her, which is partially true, and when I say I will cook her a dinner, she finds that so startling she says she will see me once more.

After spaghetti and garlic bread, we sit cross-legged on the carpet of my place. We finish a bottle of Chianti. She is mostly amazed by all the books; they testify that I am straight with her about who I am. She goes, Did you read all of them? I go, Yes. She blinks and tells me she has not read a book since required to do so in high school. She knows she should, but with this and that she has no time. Problem is, she reads too slowly; books do not tell her enough fast enough.

We are on the floor because I own almost no other furniture and she is not about to go into my bedroom to sit on the edge of my bed thank you very much. We share a second bottle, this time a cabernet, something she never before tasted. She holds her hands out to me. I see by the candlelight that her palms are worn smooth, covered by translucent, mottled unlined scar tissue.

She goes, Jack. That's all. Like the word explains everything. I go, Who in fuck is Jack? Jack is her husband. Was. She had to grasp the blade and not let go. Nothing had ever hurt so much. It was a hunting knife. There had been a lot of blood, but she was lucky; she'd pretty much kept the use of her hands and did not lose a finger. She could not sew. She missed needlepoint. Buttons can be a challenge, but zippers are all right.

Jack was in jail. She had divorced him but when he was free, they would get together again.

It was a mistake, was all. She says, "I love him."

Why had he come at her like that? What had happened? But she is not talking about that. Too personal.

So I want the video girl even more badly. I want her so I might see her brush her hair and see the curve of her bare back, and I want to see her open to me in that way that is sex and something more, but most of all I want to know what is too personal.

I show up at the video store half a dozen times more. She never smiles. Not once. Before the summer ends, she is gone. I rent *A Man For All Seasons* and learn from the new clerk, a middle-aged rummy whose hands quiver, that my video girl does not work there anymore.

Jack came at her with a hunting knife. She held the blade to save her life. She could grasp the blade and love the man. She was prey. Prey in love with her hunter. Think of it.

Hungry Like the Wolf
Duran Duran

Clasp my wrists above my head, she rasps. *Use your teeth; tenderness is wasted on me.*

Before sunup, she is gone.

Jane has appetites. Her unshaved armpits taste of salt. The wolf is Jane. This time, I will be the prey.

This will be the most carnal relationship of my life.

Don't be judgmental. *Carnal* means *flesh*, and in some places, flesh is Spirit made manifest.

In April 1985, my colleague's production of "A Midsummer Night's Dream" opens for a three night run. Four months later, I will become Jessica's fulltime custodial parent. That academic year is the only nine months of my life before I am 50 that I am single and live alone. I am 36.

Should any prospective member of the Iowa audience be unable to call to mind the author, or confuse this play with some other play by the same title, the posters around Drake University unequivocally read, "Shakespeare's A Midsummer Night's Dream." The poster depicts a bare tree from which hangs what appears to be a pair of long-johns, and it turns out that long-johns are crucial to the production. The cast wears gray union suits large enough for Mighty Joe

Young, the sleeves and legs flopping over the actors' hands and feet. No one wears shoes. Like kids running loose at a pajama party on Mom's freshly waxed wooden floor, the cast slides along the polished stage through the play's reversals and surprises, seemingly always at the brink of an inadvertent pratfall.

Silly as this sounds, the costuming works. The company has fun; so do we. Characters smitten with irresistible passion for the wrong lover wander through the enchanted forest until sunrise when Puck, the fairy who orchestrates the farce, restores reason. When he says, "What fools these mortals be," the audience sighs with the pleasure of recognition. Iowans endure all that odd language and befuddling plot for this quotable bit of the Bard's wisdom.

The April night of the debut, I am invited to the cast party. The director and her lover have been good to me. I drink sangria and smile like a feeble-minded uncle, happy to be at the party but not quite certain of my role. Then I chat with Hermia, the willful character who is given the choice of chastity or death because she will not obey her father's will.

Hermia is played by Jane.

Hermia is 22, a graduating senior majoring in Theater, so, no, she will never be able to take a class from me. Her eyes are perfectly black. Her skin is olive. She's from Chicago. She has heard from Oberon and Bottom that I run a good creative writing seminar. I don't praise everything, nor do I savage any student's work. My opinion is trusted and important, she says. She confesses to having wondered who I was on the day last fall when she saw me in slit gym shorts, shirtless, running the streets that surround the campus, having only now at the cast party made the identification. She'd asked, but did not believe that the blond runner could be a new professor. Professors are potbellied and bald. Her pointed chin is cupped in her hand, her elbow angled to the table, her black hair is cropped short as a man's for her role as the daughter of Egeus. Now offstage, like one of Geronimo's warriors, she wears a blue headband run with a silvered metallic thread. An impervious bubble closes around us. Outside, people talk and laugh, but they are barely audible within, their voices drowned out by lightning flashes of suggestion between mine and Jane's eyes.

I've watched her most of the night under stage lights, but not until she leans toward me in her carmine, sleeveless blouse realize her wiry physique is a product of deliberate work. Jane lifts weights. She adds reps, she tells me, not additional heavier plates, pursuing form, not power. I tell her I have my own bench. When I do not run, I lift. "We'll have to lift together some time," she says. With a whisper made rough by red wine, she confides in me that more than a few women on campus muse about the young professor who bicycles to class wearing a brown corduroy sport jacket, shapeless woolen ties and running shoes. Do I dance? Do I like lasagna? Can she call me?

I say, "Sure."

I am being pursued. I will be prey. This will be different. Can I love my hunter?

Before dawn that first morning, Jane silently leaves my bed. Soon after, my telephone rings. I figure it is Jane, but it isn't.

"My name is Jan."

"Jan?"

"Jane never wants to see you again. Don't bother her."

I am standing stark naked in the kitchen, the only room in the house with a phone outlet. The linoleum is ice. All I can think is that I should be making coffee and writing. I should be preparing for class. Maybe I should be doing laundry or marketing. Clothes would be good. It's hard to focus before coffee. At this peculiar time in my life, my first unmarried year, no matter what I am doing, I am fairly sure I should be doing something else. Panic at all that remains undone coils round my neck with the weight of a boa constrictor. For the next several years, as Jessica moves to the center of my life and I become her chauffeur, father, mother, cook, nurse, confidante, mentor, and disciplinarian, the snake will awaken, feed, and swell larger.

"Can I speak to Jane?"

"No. She never wants to see you again."

"That's too bad," I say and add, "I just want to hear it from her."

Jan hangs up.

Jan and Jane. It's too cute. I'd bet they wear matching outfits and cut their hair the same way.

I figure Jane and Perry are done, and I also figure that is too bad because when I return to my bed and I pull the blanket over my head, Jane's scent, loosed from the folds of the sheets, engulfs me once more, evoking the smooth, slippery feel of her hip, the taste of her neck, and the half growl, half whimper she makes when I touch her just so.

Those years, Des Moines is overrun with uncommitted lesbians. Heterosexuality is fallen out of fashion. Shamefully déclassé, straight women maintain a low profile. These days, the finer points of identity-nomenclature evade me. Perhaps "bisexual" is more accurate, though I am told by people I trust there is no such thing. So "lesbian" it is.

Five years later, ignorant of her past, I will marry a lesbian who believes she has moved beyond that part of her life, but she will relapse when I pass through a miserable decade and my omnipresent anger flares in ways that rekindle what she has suppressed. Or hidden. It's hard to say. But our marriage, Debi's revelation and reassertion of her ambivalent sexuality, and the rubble scattered in the wake of that runaway train on a narrow mountain pass is a whole other story. Be patient.

The wolf in this tale is Jane, but Jane is not the only lesbian to find her way to my Des Moines bed. Just the first.

Flash forward to the year following *A Midsummer's Night's Dream*. Phyllis, the mother of a teenage daughter, lingers to talk with me at a cocktail reception after a public reading by a guest of Drake University.

We chat, I go home, my office phone has a voice message from her by the next day. So once or twice, Phyllis and I dine at restaurants while her kid takes care of mine. Phyllis is nice enough, though her kid has that slack-jawed and vacant-eyed look of protein deprivation affected by 15-year olds who need to believe that since they have seen all life has to offer, no surprises will ever come their way. Maybe her affected boredom is her defense against her knowledge of her mother's peculiar life. One night over olives and celery, before a waiter can deliver our steaks, with a hurried confession that's mostly apology, Phyllis tells me her roommate is something more than a roommate. Phyllis nevertheless wants to sleep with me. Tonight. Her trembling hand goes to her chest. Twice she must pause to catch her breath. This is difficult for her. Can I appreciate that? She needs to remember what it is like. She says "it." Sex? A penis? Men? I have no idea, but we cancel dinner and hurry to her house, a precisely decorated Tudor with a manicured garden in a better part of town.

The roommate travels on business. The kids are at my place. Phyllis is shy in bed, tentative as a virgin. It's been seven years, she says as she lights a scented candle and pins closed a lace curtain. Seven. She hurries the act. I learn that the idea that lesbians are sexually voracious is a stupid pornographic myth, one I'd given credence because of my encounter with Jane.

A week or so later, Phyllis tells me all her friends are excited for her. *Phyllis is dating!* I do not ask how it is that all her friends are privy to this turn of events; I am not even certain "dating" properly describes what we are about, but I say nothing. Phyllis and I have been alone together three times and have had awkward sex once. The roommate has evidently already been shown the door. Phyllis' friends are middle-level bankers, lawyers and dentists, the bourgeois backbone of Iowa's sturdy professional class. Since finding a babysitter presents no problem, and since Chubby Checker is featured at the Iowa State Fair, Phyllis informs me we are going. It's a package deal—tickets, date, sitter. Turning down the privilege is not on my menu.

Two days later, Phyllis and I twist the night away beneath the stars amid kamikaze moths and horrible corndogs. Coincidentally, no fewer than three couples who are her old friends happen to be there. There is a lot of talk about what a great place Iowa is to settle down. Great schools; great people. They've heard I am a writer. One of them is a realtor and supposes he can get me a helluva deal on a helluva starter house.

I hated Chubby Checker when he was all the rage. Twenty years later, at the Iowa State Fair of 1985, he is more vile than the corndogs.

So I lose Phyllis's number, and it takes only two or three unreturned calls to my answering machine before she stops calling me. I am a shit-heel, no question.

Barbara lifts her unshod foot into my crotch under a seminar table and later tells me she enjoys threesomes, though we never arrange such a moment for her, her female friend, and me. She has wide liquid eyes, melted emeralds that either bore holes through me or stare off into space to another world. With me, she says, she prefers simplicity. "Too many parts," she says. "Besides, I do not want to share."

I come home from a movie date to find one of the my daughter's babysitters, a basketball team guard, pushing her shirt into her jeans as the league's leading rebounder, a forward, emerges from my bathroom clad only in translucent underwear. "Hey, Professor, how are you?" the forward asks, unconcerned as she snaps up her nylon Drake-blue warm-up suit puddled on the floor before my living room hearth. I spend a restless week spooling mind-movies of the Give and Go that was enacted on my flower-upholstered sofa before the fire.

My undergraduate creative writing students—men and women—all seem to write nothing but thinly disguised, sincere autobiographies about their hidden lives. A graduating journalism major comes to trust me and confesses she is worried that her hoped-for career as a sports writer will suffer if word gets out she is a lesbian. I swear, you look at her—her stance, her hair, her clothes, her gestures—you figure she could not be anything else, but I assure her no one could ever, ever guess such a thing. The word "transsexual" has no currency at the time. Ten years later, to be sure, her sexuality will likely prove to be a career boost. She walks, talks, and moves like she has balls: who'd deny her a locker room interview?

The lesbian thing pervades my time in Des Moines.

Like open sluiceways at Hoover Dam, closets gush their contents to the young professor with a daughter. He is safe and he is presumably wise. Sexual adventure and experimentation is so widespread, I write a parody about a man who claims to be a moose trapped in a man's body. He wants surgery. He wants hormones. He grows antlers. The damn thing turns good on me and is published by *Twilight Zone Magazine*, no less. My nickname is "Moose" forever after.

Decades later, I have come to believe that so many women slept with other women because the definition of "abuse" had been stretched to new limits. A joke became a cause when leaving a toilet seat up became an intolerable insult, an act that might be met with homicidal violence. Women asked: Why embrace a lover mysterious and unknowable when one can more simply love a person who mirrors the self? Same-gender sex requires much less guesswork, and since heterosexuality mostly depends on penetration and its implications about superiority, better to obviate the whole ordeal, leave procreation to breeders, plant a garden, and lead the simple life.

Lillith's complaint shaped a sexual revolution only now being matched by the necessary political accommodation. But in the '80s, Puck orchestrated mischief. Love, misdirected and unrestrained, was all about Iowa; carnality was everywhere. Mistaken lovers ran about the forest on an enchanted night. What fools these mortal be.

A day after the final night Shakespeare's lovers in long-johns are smitten by illusory passions, Jane calls my office. She and some friends plan to be in a bar in a restaurant where a local band covers whatever it can manage from the Top Forty. We'll dance.

Before I can mumble anything about propriety, Jane tells me that the actor in residence for the semester from the Royal Shakespeare Company will be there along with no fewer than two professors from the Theater Department, not to mention any number of members from the play's cast. One of them has a brother in the band. This is no date; this is the Ambulatory Actor's Tribe and Road Show displaying support for one of its own. The only way Jane and I could be more public would be to dance on the steps of Old Main on homecoming weekend at high noon. "Besides, I'll never be your student," she reminds me a second time.

I lie. I tell Jane I don't like to dance. "Everybody dances," she says. "You know what this is about. Don't go stupid on me. Nine o'clock," she says and hangs up.

What the band lacks in skill, it makes up for with volume. I nurse a rum-and-coke for most of an hour. The bar's floor and tables are highly polished pine, lacquered over with coins, stamps, campaign buttons, and strips of inlaid brass. The final dinner-rush patrons linger among us, a swell of stable Moms and Dads waiting to be seated in the restaurant itself where they will order onion rings, fried zucchini, French fried potatoes, fried mushrooms and maybe a cheeseburger. Then they'll go home, pay the sitter, watch a little late night TV, and snore between crisp sheets while cholesterol congeals thick as river mud in their arteries, but before that restful night these good Des Moines folk push salty Chex mix into their mouths and sip light beer while, walleyed, they take in the free floorshow. Those wacky college students will do just about anything, by golly.

The actor from the RSC is an aging queen who does his best American accent when he sees me. "Glad yuh made it, Per," he says, sprawls his slender body on a chair, his left leg in Texas and his right in Oklahoma, and places a sodden white handkerchief like a shroud over his face. Where his white shirt is open to midchest, he gleams with sweat. The shirt is soaked to translucence. His narrow chest heaves.

Mostly, as motionless as those good Moms and Dads, I sit and watch and kid myself into thinking I do not know what I am doing here. It's difficult to take my eyes off Hermia. There is not much opportunity to talk.

When the houselights dim at 11:00, the dinner crowd is gone and the electric candles are dimmed to a dull orange. The band swings into its version of the hit of the moment, *Hungry Like the Wolf*. The recording features a snare drum, a panting woman, and lyrics that are single entendre. *I'm on a hunt, I'm after you.* The members of the wildly popular band, Duran Duran, are decidedly androgynous. There is no subtlety in this tune.

And there is Jane, bending toward me, shoulders shaking, her black spaghetti-strap top gapping open, her hanging breasts shimmering inches from my eyes.

213

She licks her lips, her eyes are half-closed. I can smell her perfume. That bubble forms again. She's been knocking back vodka and 7-Up as if it were Gatorade.

"I really don't like sweating," I say, and think of my high school students, years ago, supple and young.

"Stop trying to be cool. When bodies dance, bodies sweat," says the acting major who is comfortable with her instrument. By my two hands, she pulls me to my feet. She presses herself into my back.

You feel my heat I'm just a moment behind....

I howl and I whine, I'm after you.
Mouth is alive all running inside
And I'm hungry like the wolf.

Jane can dance. That night, so do I. I go home near 1:30, and half an hour later, Jane appears at my door. Without a word, she wraps her leg around my hip, standing, and when her lips open, she does taste like wine.

The next morning, I hear from Jan, but that turns out to mean nothing much.

Months later on the late July day Jessica arrives in her mother's van, they are 24 hours early, having driven all night across half a continent to save a motel bill. It's 3:00 in the afternoon. Jane is in town for a few days, having graduated weeks before. We are in my bed when the truck's gears grind up the driveway, Jane watching herself perform in my bedside mirror, and we hear the engine die as Jane completes a ninety-minute blow-job so perfect I think I may levitate to peer into the face of God. We hurriedly dress. While Helena's husband and Jane share a joint in the backyard, I show Jessica and her mother what will be Jessica's room. The irony that Helena and I are with partners who are near the same age, a decade or so younger than either of us, is not lost on Helena.

We are capable of pretending that the decade we were married did not happen despite the evidence of Jessica's existence. All we need to do is glance at our lovers, evidence no time has been lost. I'm having an adventure with a young woman; Helena is throwing the dice again, reclaiming a lost decade of her life.

Jessica, however, has not had a good year. She is very excited to be joining me.

The four of us empty the van of Jessica's furniture, struggling to pass pieces up a narrow spiral staircase. We hurry. Once the furniture is unloaded, they will push on to a family reunion in Wisconsin. Jessica will go with them. I will return Jane to Chicago, then scoot north to gather up Jessica no earlier than August 1. Helena will head back to Arizona, but before returning to Des Moines and a new school year, Jessica and I will head further east to New York City.

It's a bad, bad time for Helena; she's giving up her daughter. As part of our performance for Jessica's sake, though they refuse to spend the night, the five of us decide to go to dinner; Jessica, her mother, her new husband, me, and my not-lately-lesbian fellatrix who enjoys light bondage, being bitten, and having her hair pulled. I cannot bring myself to slap her as hard as she wants me to.

Burgers all around.

The most carnal relationship of my life will last not quite four months more, six total, intermittent encounters to enjoy acrobatic sex that argue for fucking to become an Olympic event. I don't suggest "competitive"; I have in mind the ancient Olympics, the celebration of the best that is human. In ancient Greece, a cadre of gods and goddesses acted upon enmity, lust, love, and passion, even as you and I. Those deities perspired. Nothing equaled Greek worship of human form in marble for two thousand years until Michelangelo liberated with a chisel the sacred and profane figures he saw imprisoned in alabaster. But my time with Jane was unrelated to worship or art. There was nothing sacred to it. Certainly, no ritual. We collided like Andrew Marvell's am'rous birds of prey, though to be sure Jane was no coy mistress.

In Iowa, I learned to cook, mend clothes, and to show up at open school night while feigning interest. I also tasted pure carnality.

And then Jane suddenly rediscovered Mother Church, a turn in her life she tells me requires her to abandon girls and Jews. The carnality of her college years needed to be behind her—either that or at 22 she figured out the last thing she needed was a man 300 miles away who was fourteen years her senior and had a child born when she was five. The truth of Jane's motives doesn't matter.

What matters is that we shared an unrestrained

howl and whine. I was the prey on that hunt. I felt the heat; Jane was close behind.

That April night in Iowa when Jane dances, I dance with her. We dance like my Brooklyn high school students danced, from the ankles up, filled with juice and joy. At Jane's request, the band plays *Hungry Like the Wolf* two, three times. They have no female vocalist, so Jane leans into me at the bridge and on cue pants. We bump, grind, and dip; we lean, forward and back; we spin, bend, swerve; we sway, hands on, hands off, hands on again. Circling an invisible center, we become slippery with sweat. Jane's rich lips stay parted, her eyes half closed. She presses herself into my back, her breath hot on me, the point of her tongue a quick flick to the soft skin beneath my ear. Her arms rest on my shoulders. When she turns me to face her, I lose myself in her infinite inky eyes, dark and wet as those Iowa nights.

Puck had it wrong.

Mortal love is never foolish.

Jessica
The Allman Brothers

July, air thick as soup but clear as cold water, I step hard on a spade's edge and push it into Iowa's rich black dirt. Setting a tetherball court will be tougher than I thought.

To dig a hole, you build a hill.

My back reminds me why I have made a life where I work with my mind. I wipe my face with the red bandana I have tied at my throat. I am shirtless, 37, wearing blue running shorts and cheap nylon running shoes.

A few yards from me on the cracked driveway, neatly stacked in a squat pyramid, are three bags of concrete mix. Now that my back and arms feel the labor, I realize I have purchased enough mix to set the landing strip for an F-14 fighter jet. But I want this thing to be solid. Yesterday, a muscular kid whose broad easy grin exposed a mouth full of white, even teeth, carried the bags to my yellow Chevette, waited while I opened the hatchback, and dropped the bags into the rear. The car sagged. The kid told me he plays left tackle for his high school; he carried all three bags under one arm and called me "sir." At home, with two hands, I strained at each bag one at a time to unload the Chevette. The kid made me feel old.

I wondered if I might preset everything into a coffee can, but decide that isn't sufficiently stable. Not for Jessica. My kid needs stable.

The garden-hose water tastes of rubber. The sun spills fire on my back; tomorrow my shoulders and neck will radiate heat. After some time digging, I scrupulously follow the printed directions, mixing precise proportions of cement, sand, gravel, and water directly into the hole. Concrete is cement added to other stuff. Cement eventually crumbles; concrete lasts forever.

When it comes to my child, I am a concrete kind of guy.

Perspiration flows in rivulets down my forearms. Once my terrycloth tennis wristlets are saturated, the shovel handle becomes slick. A blister rises on my thumb; another swells across my palm. Prior blisters on my hand were raised by a tennis racket. My hands are the soft hands of a writer who teaches.

I hold the short stub of the tetherball post erect while the concrete base thickens. The post base is nothing more than a short length of slender pipe. I prop it erect with a few spare bricks. The next morning, after I set the kit's five-foot extension pole onto the stubby base, I tie a clothesline rope to the post top and attach the tetherball to the other end of the line. Then I run at the post, hitting it as if it were a tackling dummy. It bends, then springs erect.

In such ways, I make myself ready.

The house I'd rented was walking distance from the center of Drake University. My contract renewed for a second year of three, they will pay me to teach Creative

Writing. Jessica, eight, will join me on August 1. The plan for the next few years is for her to stay one school year with her mother, the next with me, alternating until she is too old for that to make sense.

It's a plan about which the Arizona court had been skeptical. The divorce court judge had questioned me closely about Helena's and my joint custody plan, especially since Helena had chosen not to appear at the proceeding, but rather than risk a postponement, I'd pleaded her case. Helena had a degree in counseling, I pointed out, and I'd been a high school teacher for a decade.

The judge reluctantly agreed. "If any people can pull this off, I guess you can."

My first Des Moines apartment on the third floor in the adults-only wing of a three-building complex in West Des Moines had a terrace that overlooked the tennis courts, barbecue area, and swimming pool. Coming off the divorce, I had some notion I would live like Hugh Hefner. But the only people in the pool were young kids on inflated rafts being carefully monitored by mothers in caftans who lived in the two other buildings. In late summer evenings, their husbands joined them. The husbands did not wear caftans, but appeared in late afternoons wearing madras shorts, sandals, and black business socks that rose to cover their pale calves. Entire Iowa families burned beef on shared grills. Neighbors lingered over yellow and pink Tupperware tubs of macaroni salad and German potato salad and tossed green salad and fruit-laced Jell-O salad with pecans, store-bought coleslaw and Ambrosia, a sticky-sweet concoction made of sour cream, coconut, mandarin oranges, and God knows what else. You could mortar drywall or power the Queen Mary on a spoonful of the stuff, and hearty Iowans ingested it by the bucket. No, it wasn't dessert. It was a side dish on a paper plate, right beside the cheesy mashed potatoes. Tapioca pudding—now that was dessert.

It's easy to make fun, but love of family is not the same as what I knew of love, that mix of carnality that can conjoin spirit. The New York sharpie learned from those good people. Perhaps our language is inadequate. Why don't we have as many words for love as Eskimos have for snow? Maybe *ambrosia* is the right word—a concoction that is sweet, hearty, and sticks to the ribs.

I am in ambrosia with Jessica. We would grow fat with it.

After Jessica's ten-day December visit, I rethink my living arrangements. West Des Moines turned out to have so little in common with the Playboy Mansion that days after I wave goodbye to Jessica's taxiing jet, I turn to my employer for help. The guy who runs faculty housing for Drake University looks like an insurance agent—everyone in Des Moines looks like an insurance agent. But despite his obvious disapproval of my youth, my divorce, and the fact that I own no pair of solid, black wingtips, that good man took pity on the bachelor professor about to become a single parent. My daughter and I are offered the big house at 1327 32nd Street. One block from campus on an oak and sycamore-lined street, wedged between a McDonald's and a seldom-used parking lot, not quite in hailing distance of Fraternity Row, it's a tad shabby and redolent with Big Macs, but the fact is I have lucked out, and I know it.

Large enough for a family of six at least, the house's single honey oak-paneled room that is the entire second floor will be Jessica's. Flanking her three dormer windows are five walk-in closets, ceilings so low I stoop to enter. These closets are hospitable only to munchkins, bridge trolls, hobbits and 8-year-old girls. The attic's double windows are set above cedar window seats; each pair of windows faces another compass point. In the aging kitchen downstairs, though the house is unoccupied when I look it over, the refrigerator is running. The freezer compartment is thick with ice; I foresee that if I take this place, like my mother in my earliest memories, to defrost the thing I will regularly boil pots of water and chip at accumulated frost with a screwdriver and a hammer.

Betty Crocker would faint dead away, but the kitchen will serve as a place to make spaghetti, the limit of my culinary skill. I am sworn to never defrost or open a can to feed Jessica. The bathroom tub's clawed feet rest on cracked pink tile. The pipes deliver so little water pressure that someone has screwed a bit of rubber hose to the tub faucet as what I figure is a shampoo rinse. That trickle might also work as a bidet, but this seems less important. There is no shower. The dining room's honest-to-heaven glass chandelier is fuzzy with dust, and the two first-floor bedrooms, like the attic dancehall that will be my kid's room, have hardwood floors so uneven that my furniture's legs will require cardboard shims. My barbells and a weight bench can live in the rear bedroom; the front bedroom will barely hold my queen-size platform bed. To walk between it and the mirrored panel doors of the closet, I will have to sidle sideways. The living room's brick and stone fireplace rivals Citizen Kane's, and in that room the green wall-to-wall carpet is thread-worn, but serviceable. Opposite the hearth, beyond a pair of French doors, surely constructed before the parking lot was paved over, perhaps when that land was a copse of trees, someone long ago added a sunroom, no more than an alcove really, with floor-to-ceiling glass on one wall and floor-to-ceiling oak bookshelves and dozens of tiny drawers on the other two. Water stains and dusty outlines of books betray the position of plants and volumes long gone. In that sunroom at my desk, I imagine pounding away on my SCM 220 Automatic Typewriter. I will I smoke my pipe, and, pausing between great thoughts, contemplate the mighty trees that like sentinels line the street, the place where I will in the smithy of my soul forge the consciousness of my race, but unlike James Joyce will do so absent any Nora Barnacle.

How could evil visit such a place? I'd rent the sunroom alone. Stalwart families cohered and grew strong in this solid house. I think: *Live, love, work.* Yes, this will do. Maybe I will learn to mix ambrosia.

So several months ahead of Jessica's arrival, I move in. That February, my heating bill tops $600 because the wind whistles through the rattling windowpanes where caulk long ago dried to powder. Drake is not about to invest in storm windows on a structure sure to be demolished in the near future. The heating system in the unpaved basement looks like a Hindu god with fourteen serpents for arms; I approach it with trepidation and a spray can of WD-40. The ducts all deliver heated air to somewhere in the house above. I open and twist rusted valves that squeal complaints at the unaccustomed movement, experimenting until I discover a configuration that establishes something above arctic temperatures in Jessica's attic room. I stock hardwood for the living room hearth. That fireplace is not about romance; it's about not quaking with cold.

The house teaches me to cook, dust, vacuum, polish, and launder; when I steer a cart through the local market, the spirits of the parents who provided for their kids in the big Iowa house guide my arm to Ajax, Clorox and Pine Sol, brand names I know from my childhood. Doing my marketing, I hum thirty-year-old advertising jingles.

The ever-earnest Midwest works its spell on me. This is a good place. I am told that Iowa's black dirt is the most fertile in the world, and comes spring everyone urges me to start a garden. I know less about gardening than I know about farming—and I know nothing about farming at all. Setting a pole in concrete in this soil from which anything can grow, the soil that nourishes the world, is for the entire three years I live in Iowa my sole gesture to agriculture.

This second summer in Iowa for me will be Jessica's first. I pick her up as agreed in Wisconsin, we visit family in New York, humping the four cylinder un-air-conditioned yellow Chevette back and forth across the Mississippi and up and down the Appalachians. We stay at motels that advertise HBO and swimming pools. We listen to godawful tapes of kid books, Jessica reading along by turning pages at the beep. One version of *Treasure Island* is so wretched we mutually agree to stop the car on an interstate shoulder in Indiana, unravel the filament of tape to watch it float and flutter over a cornfield, and then we trample the plastic cassette. When I pour hot coffee from a thermos while I drive, it invariably spills into my crotch, a moment Jessica finds hilarious. We eat road food, pecan rolls from Stuckey's and any fudge with nuts. Jessica takes long naps in the rear seat. I make hopeless passes at waitresses, and when back in the car Jessica feigns humiliation, I tell her it is just to stay in practice. We make 600 miles in a day and never have better times.

Returned to Des Moines, I unlock the door. Stale house air washes over us, a puff of angel's breath. We haul our luggage through the door with the unmistakable sense of returning home.

That first evening, after we unpack, buy basic groceries, eat, and walk to the spot where next week Jessica will board the school bus, we climb the wooden spiral stairs to her room. The final light of day is murky. I did not repair the broken light switch; the only working illumination is a yellowish bulb with a pull chain at the ceiling's center. I put clean linen on her familiar bed.

"Before you sleep," I say, "your room needs to be aired out."

So we kneel on the cedar window-seats beside each other to open the narrow casement windows that face the house's front. The catch is shellacked shut. A streetlight beyond the big tree in the front yard casts its light through the lush leaves; shadows flit over our faces. I rap the window frame with my palm until it cracks loose, swings on its side hinges, and then gapes open. Sweet night air washes over us.

"Something flew in the window," Jessica says.

"Don't be silly. Look what a pretty night it is."

"I'm scared." She clutches at my arm.

It annoys me that she summons up spooks from darkness. I say, "All right. We'll have some milk and cookies while the room airs out, and when we come back, we'll close the window and the shade so there are no shadows. How's that?"

Later, I lean against the bathroom doorframe to watch Jessica brush her teeth, awkward for her because she is too short to see the mirror. She'll need a stepstool; I suppose there will have to be other fine adjustments. I barely forgive myself. Okay, so no one thinks of everything. We will become reacquainted. The trip we finished was good, but to know each other in this new living arrangement we will need to create new routines. In the year we have been separated, despite the December visit, Jessica has grown and changed so much I hardly know her. She holds sensible conversations, understands irony, and is capable of originating sarcasm.

Five days on the road had transformed my spine to a column of cracked marble, and hours of unpacking left me stupid with boredom. "Hold my hand," I say after climbing the stairs to her now pitch dark room. The broken switch moves up in my priorities. We set out to cross the vast, empty space, my arm waving before my face until it finds the string tied to the light's chain. I tug it.

Jessica begins shrieking.

The bat that hangs a few feet above her bed casts a very long shadow across the ceiling. Some spooks in the darkness are real.

"Under your blankets. Quick."

Kneeling, her head beneath her pillow, her little behind in the air, she covers herself. Don't bats entangle in girls' hair? Are they rabid? I grab the broom with which we swept and swiped at cobwebs.

Heavy as a ripe pineapple, the bat is the biggest damn thing I've ever seen. It may as well be fucking Bela Lugosi. I swing the broom, and however in hell bats see—radar? sonar?—it flutters away. Leather wings soft as Death whisper over my face.

"Stay under!"

I swing and miss again. "You son-of-a-bitch!" Ahab spat at Moby Dick with less venom. With every swing, I bellow profanity. I yell to Jessica to stay covered. Desperate, I whirl around the room flailing a straw broom at the air.

And then the broom finds it.

The bat falls to the floor where it spasms, broken. I

hit it again to be sure it is immobile, and then I press the life from it by leaning all my weight on the broom.

Unspent adrenaline leaves my arms trembling. The muscles in my neck and shoulders knot. Tomorrow, they will ache.

I bend close. The thing I killed is no larger than my palm, a three-inch mouse with wings, its eyes tiny slits, its frail wings broken. *What the hell have I done?*

"Come out," I say.

We stand over the tiny corpse. I pant as though I've run a mile, and I am covered with as much sweat. Without touching the bat, we manage to slide the body onto my tennis racket and carry it to the still open window. I hurl the bat into the darkness, and I slam shut and latch Jessica's window.

"I told you something flew in," Jessica says and asks me to look away while she puts on her pajamas.

With my back to her, I say something idiotic about bad words and how people use them when they are frightened. When Jessica has the blanket tucked under her chin, because it is something that I am sure good parents in good places like Iowa do, I try to read her a story. I am planning *Lord of the Rings*, the entire trilogy. Then *Narnia*. Every book. She will have none of it, though; not this first night in our new place.

"Are there lots of bats in Iowa?"

"I've never seen one before. I think they mostly live in caves."

"You really, really screamed."

The next morning, we search for the dead bat, but during the night, something took it. We never find a trace. I keep thinking how small it was, how large it seemed.

Jessica was indeed named for the Allman Brother's tune: it's on *Brothers and Sisters*, an album that was released in 1973 when the band changed its sound to include a piano, a necessity because too many of its guitar players were turning themselves into road-kill by skidding into intersections on speeding motorcycles. At the time of Jessica's birth, Helena and I were at our hungriest for a taste of what we thought was the real America.

Dicky Betts composed the wordless tune for his young daughter, and long after its release, it won a special Grammy Award, compensation for an oversight twenty years after the fact. The music is distilled joy.

Jessica was a popular name in 1975. No matter where she went to school, my daughter forever had a classmate with the same name. Before her birth, Helena and I had fabricated the name Deena, and, for a while, we thought "Deena Jessica" would be it. I assumed she'd be forever "DJ," but at the last minute, as we did with so many things, we chickened out from the truly unconventional and settled for what was traditional. So our daughter was named Jessica Deena Glasser. A year after her birth, taking a cue from the Allman Brothers band, I abandoned my own motorcycling. I have a photo of Jessica on my candy-ass blue Honda; she's less than a year old, a pair of mirrored aviator sunglasses balanced on her radiant face.

Jessica and I were together three days in Iowa when I realize she was being noble to spare my feelings. Wrapped in a green towel, her bare shoulders still shining with bath water, she sat with her back to me. Like her mother's, my 8-year-old daughter's hair fell several inches below her shoulders. I worked the brush along the line her part should follow, pushed the brush to her scalp, tugged, and my kid tried not to cry out. She did whimper.

The brush was tangled in her hair.

It was not courage that kept her silent. Jessica's last hope for a place that could be hers was with me, and so she would not complain. Her mother and her husband had given her up. What could Jessica know of divorce decrees? Until that moment the hairbrush tangled, I'd not realized the degree to which Jessica was at some psychological risk. The insight kicked me all hollow. She'd endure any amount of pain rather than allow Daddy to think she needed attention. What if Daddy did not want her, either?

Planning for Jessica's arrival, I'd mentally projected our lives far into the future, especially those terrifying, predictable, firsts: first bra, first period, first—and only—time coming home puking drunk, the inevitable beau who would be an acne-ridden drooling idiot quitting high school to pursue a career as a professional kickboxer. Mind you, I had no clue what I would do about most of those events (though the kickboxer scenario had a definite script involving a crowbar), but I could at least delude myself into believing that when those moments arrived I might by then have accumulated some wisdom.

I'd planned hot breakfasts against the Iowa winters. I stocked up on oatmeal. My vision swam with dreams of cookies close beside a full glass of milk. The recipe was right there on the oatmeal package! What could there be to it? I dedicated myself to being sure Jessica's clothing would be ironed crisp and washed spotless, for which purpose I'd bought a washer and dryer within days of moving from the apartment to the house. I practiced ironing and, shortly after Jessica arrived, deduced that the inventor of pleats was either a sadist or a Victorian with a fulltime laundress. Jessica's complexion would be creamy, she'd never, ever, catch cold, and her hair would be forever lustrous.

That goddam hairbrush was knotted about two inches from her scalp above her ear, five inches from the tangled ends of her hair and a light-year from all I had imagined. Perfect father? More likely, Jessica would be tortured to baldness by her old man, the Barber from Buchenwald. I recalled my mother telling my sister it took a little pain to be beautiful, but uprooting Jessica's hair from her scalp seemed too great a price to pay. Maybe I was fit to ride with Sitting Bull and Crazy Horse, but fatherhood?

I gave up. I carefully scissored out the brush, taking as little hair as possible. Jessica's hair dried where it fell, unbrushed. Within days, her head became a place that looked like a bird's nest in molting season. She was perfectly happy looking like a child raised by wolves. When her hair grew longer, I planned to buy her a big honkin' hat.

Parenting. Simplicity itself.

When Jessica joined me in Iowa she had no cold weather wardrobe. Autumn did not exist in Tucson, but in Des Moines shortly after school started, she needed jeans, a coat, and sweatshirts.

Whether in Iowa or Irkutsk, I advise any father who stands outside the try-on room in the Girl's Department not to peer anxiously toward the entrance. Mothers get to pass beyond the curtains into the little cubical rooms; Dads are sequestered near the entrance because good family-oriented people are wary of creeps who stare at half-dressed children.

That afternoon, I shrug off the glares from women who eyeball the man pushing his hand through racks of girls' clothing, but there is no ignoring the mall security rent-a-cop who politely, but firmly, asks to have a few words with me. I suppose the biddy who'd alerted the guard to the perv in the kids' department was in the small group of onlookers. "What do you think you are doing?" the guy asks me as he hitches his pants.

I have no idea what is going on. Did I leave my lights on in the parking lot? I tell him I am shopping.

"But you keep staring into the try-on room. What do you hope you'll see?"

Jessica chooses that moment to emerge in salmon pink size 6X jeans. I ask her to turn around to examine how the seat fits. From the corner of my eye, I see a woman turn away, and it finally dawns on me what this little show of community concern is about. The seat is baggy, but with the onlookers and the guard watching my every move I do not dare grab at my kid's bottom to see how much loose material is there. The mood of the Midwest, that innocent gesture might have bought me hard time. But since Jessica is obviously a happy kid, clean except for a head of hair that might be jungle undergrowth, the guard lets it drop. I receive no apology, of course.

All this episode meant was that I would be caught red-handed another day.

Single fathers are presumed guilty until proven innocent; even after proof of innocence, the lousy bastards are probably guilty of something, somewhere. A murdered wife must be buried in some unmarked field; children must have been ripped from the loving embrace of a mother persecuted by a politically connected father chummy with judges, DAs and the FBI. You have seen the TV movies about the mothers' undergrounds; you've read the headlines about the abusive fathers. Mere facts cannot obstruct marketing opportunities—and it is women who buy products. They are called *soap operas* for a reason. There are men who watch soap operas, and there are men who buy laundry soap, but should you become chief of marketing for Proctor and Gamble, do not allow your enlightened attitudes to obstruct your drive for profit. You will see few inspirational *Lifetime* movies about how the heartwarming challenges of single fatherhood may be overcome without the intervention of a loving woman, though you can find plenty of TV shows and films about bachelor dads whose incompetence is a cause for hilarity.

In real life, the life you and I live, the search for validation, autonomy, and love pardons all bad behaviors by women. Mothers may shed their kids like old hosiery because they seek a fresh start with a new man, and some pitiable crazed witch will drown her kids in her car, but any rendering of that drama must also suggest she was first victimized by a man who drove her mad. Lacking any evidence for a motive other than madness, the suppressed memory of her father or uncle waving his weenie can be unearthed or invented. Why else would a woman hang her kids in the attic and shoot the dog before burning down the house?

Weeks before the shopping mall shakedown, I registered Jessica in school. On school's first day, as we walk the tree-lined Des Moines streets we are joined by dozens of decent-looking kids. Jessica glows. She is back with Daddy; she will be attending a new school. Several houses on the route display a poster of a blue leaf in a front window or behind the screen that encloses a front porch; days later Jessica informs me that Blue Leaf houses are approved safe havens. Any kid in trouble or who needs a bathroom can stop there.

Terrific! What an idea! I call the school to ask if my house can be a Blue Leaf house. I want to be part of my new community. Forms come by mail; I fill them out. A few days later, I am rejected.

I am unmarried. "Policy," the police sergeant explains when I call. "Don't take it personally."

In that first October in Iowa, comes sweater weather and sunshine, I suggest it might be a good day to learn to ride a two-wheeler. Jessica's battered bike with training wheels and a banana seat is in the heap among her still unsorted possessions. I wrestle it down the narrow winding stairs, scratching stairwell wood panels all the way.

Before our house on the street deep with fallen leaves, Jessica confesses that she is defective, incapable of learning to ride a bike. Her mother's husband tried to teach her, she tells me, but after a day of him yelling at her, he put the training wheels back on. She has not been on the bike since that day. She adds, "Now the bike is broken." Jessica's hands are deep in her jeans pockets. Her burgundy cardigan sweater is zipped to her chin, the collar rolled under her long, wild hair.

I look more closely. The training wheels are missing a bolt; a second screw has been stripped. The machine wobbles and rattles, and the left training wheel is frozen in place. The pink paint is chipped and the foxtail that flew defiantly from a whip-antenna is gone. I recall the Strawberry Shortcake bike shining new, a happy time now long ago and far away.

"I can't learn to ride a bike," she says for the third time. "I just can't."

I squat to equalize our heights. I see the woe in her eyes. So I stow her bicycle on the tiny porch, removing the reminder of her failure, and then in one of those inspired moments every parent prays for, I suggest a special lunch. The prospect of food brightens Jessica's mood, and when I name the sandwich shop, Beggar's

Banquet, a grain-bread and sprouts place on the opposite side of the university campus, she knows that the good creamy carrot cake is in her future.

There is, however, one condition.

She watches doubtfully as I wrestle my ancient crap-brown Rudge with all of five gears off the porch to the sidewalk. The kid seat I had over the rear wheel in Arizona is long gone. Jessica would have been too large for it, anyway. I straddle the Rudge and lift her to the frame top bar. She sits sidesaddle between my arms. I caution her to keep her feet in, but not so far as to let them touch the spinning front wheel. "Hold the handle bars," I say, and before she can object, we push off.

Tart autumn air paints color onto her face. Dry leaves follow in our wake. It's Saturday, the deserted campus poses no navigation problems, there are no autos, and we ride in broad swooping circles over walkways that hug gentle hills. Secure between my arms, Jessica shrieks with delight. Her hair lashes back to sting my face.

Later that week, we discard her rattling training wheels. With a little 10W-40, she now has a genuine two-wheeler. After two hours of my running beside her gripping her banana seat, she learns to ride and, *voila!* she is no longer defective. The woman I will in a few years marry, Debi, and I follow Jessica on an untrafficked street, and when we shout, "Pedal, pedal, pedal!" to help her conquer a small rise, Jessica irritably calls back to us, "Stop encouraging me!"

Some advantages to being single and a father are

less than spiritual. I discover any number of women who take the sight of a happy, well-adjusted girl to be an indicator that a man probably does not keep thumbscrews or a rack in his basement. A bachelor with a happy child vaults to a trust level otherwise unapproachable for weeks. Moreover, an unattached man and a child fulfill a definite fantasy for some younger women, allowing them a little harmless role-playing. Some play the role as far as possible.

I never exploited Jessica in that way, at least not by design; however, the phenomenon is here duly observed.

Back then, mostly I am broke. When I invite a woman for a late evening dinner it is because I cannot afford a babysitter or much else. Once it is clear I actually intend to cook instead of ordering out for pizza, these evenings turn satisfactory for all concerned.

Jessica's nature and our situation require that she meet my friend of the moment before she allows herself to be put to bed. I become selective about partners. I have never had any taste for haunting some meat market to sip a gin and tonic while waiting for another lonely soul, so I meet women where I can. We stay sober and we talk. Sometimes I have a baby sitter and am out in the evening, but more often I find companionship in perfectly ordinary places. Once it is agreed that a meal at my place together might be all right, after the wine and coffee, we might read to Jessica. The kid will insist on a kiss goodnight, and some young women have their socks charmed off. Maybe more than their socks.

Smart, social, and more than a little precocious, Jessica learns discretion. At breakfast, she never asks about the other lady, the one who made better scrambled eggs or who did not burn the toast. By the time she is nine, Jessica shares with me her insights about which of my dinner partners had what feminine virtues, and by ten she blackmails me with threats to reveal everything unless her allowance is raised. Small bribes exchange hands.

Her psychological health seems unimperiled by my behavior. It's not as though I am bedding five women per week; more like five in a year. My job is to be Dad; her job is to be the kid. Grown-ups do what grown-ups do; kids do what kids do. Parts of my life are private; parts of her life are private. We respect that, and she respects that I am in charge of drawing those boundaries. Jessica is confident of my attention's return soon enough.

We learn our jobs, Kid and Dad. That's a very small, very tight, wholly satisfactory family.

However, Jessica does feel the weight of presumed guilt people want to place on me, her bachelor father. No one can get permission to attend her pajama party: who'd put their daughter in a house where the only adult was a man? Then there was the Saturday afternoon birthday gathering at a friend's house. At the front door, I am greeted by a woman stiff as a Switzer at the Vatican greeting the Antichrist. Jessica slips by to join the crowd of screaming kids, but I can only crane my neck to see into the kitchen where a circle of adult woman schmooze and drink coffee. "Come back in a few hours," the hostess says to me. Banished, I run a few miles and return at the appointed time, not thinking much about the situation, but in our car Jessica tells me that there had been a party game for the girls *and* their mothers. "It sucked," she says. "They would not let me play." She thinks a moment more. "It was a really stupid game."

Early on, Jessica saw right to the principle of a thing.

That first Iowa April, the day before Jessica is to fly off to her mother for the weeklong spring recess, she informs me she wants to remain with me the following school year. "That's something your mother has to hear from you," I say, "so you be sure to tell her when you see her." If I telephone Helena and break this news, she will be looking for Jessica's photo on milk cartons.

Jessica works up all her courage of eight-and-a-half years. She asks me for advice; I tell her to say what she feels. I also caution her that whatever her mother decides is the way it will have to be. I add that her mother and I have only her best interests in mind. Jessica is not some emblem or a trophy, and I share this with Jessica believing it with a full heart. Helena was a lot of things, but none of them made her ruthless with her daughter.

As it turns out, events in her mother's life make Jessica's request for a change in plans timely. Helena and her husband expect their first child. After two years together, they are flat broke, having bankrupted the business Helena's father bought them and having sold both the houses Helena owned in Tucson. Maybe it went up their noses: who can guess? Since no money follows Jessica's physical custody, and since there is no possibility of receiving child support, Helena consents to Jessica's request.

Helena eventually has two sons. What was to have been for Jessica and me an exception of two consecutive years became permanent.

But back in Iowa, that first year at about the time of the Great Bicycle Triumph, I take Jessica to a walk-in mall beautician. Her hair worries me. She looks like Harpo Marx. I expect phone calls from concerned guidance counselors discreetly asking about neglect.

Jessica lies with her head tilted back over a sink. She wears a checkered blue jumper. I chat with the hairdresser while her long fingers work shampoo through Jessica's hair. After the rinse, I carefully watch her brush it out, starting at the ends and working her way toward Jessica's scalp, freeing tangles until she easily and smoothly—and painlessly—can run a comb its full length.

You start at the ends, dimwit, not the scalp.

"What cream rinse does she use?" the woman asks me.

Cream rinse?

In time, ever more mysteries are dispelled.

Being the Knight who rescued the Princess from the Dragon is the single best role of my life. Its purity is not questionable. Years have passed since the time when Jessica and I crisscrossed America every summer in my tiny two-door car spilling coffee into my crotch because I am unwilling to allow her to try her hand at pouring hot fluids, and I am too driven to do anything as reasonable as pulling over to the roadside. Though a number of my oldest friends and their wives have flattered me about my willingness to do what so few men try, I don't think that accepting single fatherhood was noble. And when my male friends tell me in confidence they are sure they could not have done what I did, I assure them they are wrong.

I can write many more pages about Jessica, of course, but after our initial years as a family of two, by the time she turned 11 and we headed for Massachusetts, she was much her own person.

There came days during her adolescence I'd have happily strangled her. Jessica had her share of predictable difficulties, but none were planet killers. I'd seen those strike my high school students. Whenever Jessica seemed to be drifting toward a dreadful course, I'd remember those girls, and instead of stiffening my neck, I'd loosen up.

Raising a daughter is like extricating yourself from Chinese fingercuffs: the trick is not to pull harder, but to relax. I'd seen unreasoned, silent, secret resistance. It is what girls do. If I was so right about the dangers of a course of action, then Jessica's good sense would come to her rescue, not me or some rule that felt arbitrarily imposed to her.

As advice, that seems anti-intuitive. I had few rules, other than to deny her any experience that has a significant chance of a *nonreversible* outcome. That philosophy held true through most of her adolescence. As an adult, Jessica is unafraid of prudent risk.

Having been a teacher in an all-girls' school, my notion of nonreversible is probably more narrow than safety-obsessed America. Look, if a girl passes 16 able to walk, talk, read, write, and has not carried a child to term, it's time to open a bottle of the better cognac and raise a glass all around. There are no guarantees against the catastrophes of chance, but we cannot keep our children locked away from life, either.

Safe children experiment, but not all experiments meet with success. Failed experiments are as valuable as successes, maybe more. In both cases, good sense grows. It is desperate girls who denied freedom crash and burn.

"Safe" means that when they fall off a bike, they are confident they will be caught. If their hair tangles, they need to know it can be tamed. They need to know they will be protected from whatever real or imagined thing that flies in unseen from the night. They need to know that when they come down the gangway, they will be met at the airport. Confident of food, shelter, and clothing, girls learn to be bold, form opinions, and welcome risk. Probably boys, too, but I do not know about that.

As a parent, I planned my own obsolescence. Jessica grew into a precocious, smart and funny kid who grew into a creative, smart and funny woman. She is accomplished and ladylike, unless she is around me — at which time she becomes as foul-mouthed as a Brooklyn boy in a poolroom. I like the woman she is. That's worth saying, and probably all that needs to be said.

The stories of Jessica's later days are hers to tell, not mine.

Twenty years after we depart the Heartland, I pass through Kansas City on business. Des Moines is close by, a mere two hours due north on I-35, the kind of side-trip that in the Midwest seems trivial.

It is June. I make the drive to visit my ex.

It seems to me the city has doubled in size, at least. Corporate America discovered a central location with good golf courses, top-notch public schools, and an educated work force that liked to work. Like any other fool who revisits his past, I think how I should have been buying distressed farmland. The city had to grow somewhere, right?

I promised myself I would not, but before I return south to Kansas City and my departing jet, I drive to 1327 32nd Street. The gray stucco house still stands. The oak and sycamores still arch over the narrow street, cooling the block with deep shade. I roll down the car window; fresh late spring air rolls in, a pillow of soft air.

I am in my early 50s. I recall July nights smoking cigarettes on the narrow front cement steps, the musty smell of the cut hardwood stacked on the porch, how in winter the frozen logs popped and sizzled when they were in the fire, being housebound after a blizzard, rushing into the street to steal a look at the eerie green sky when sirens sounded a tornado warning, a crazy city-boy without enough common sense to seek shelter from a whirlwind.

I crack my car door open, crouch, and skulk unseen like a burglar under the windows up the narrow driveway, pausing only to run my fingertips over the marred rat-gray paint at the spot where I once scraped a car's fender. The scar is still there, though the exposed plaster is no longer white and raw. At the driveway's end, I confirm what my heart already knows.

In the small backyard's center, three or four inches higher than the overgrown grass near a stand of rhubarb, a six-inch pipe protrudes from the earth. I try it with my foot.

Solid.

Somebody to Love
Jefferson Airplane

When the truth is found to be lies
and all the joys within you dies

Don't you want somebody to love
don't you need somebody to love
wouldn't you love somebody to love
you better find somebody to love

When the garden flowers baby are dead yes
and your mind is full of red

Don't you want somebody to love?

I

The contributions from Debi's salary to our accounts have inexplicably gone uncredited. We hemorrhage cash. The checkbook won't add up.

Some flunky at the mutual fund company insists the money was never sent. I snarl, "It's an automatic deduction, moron! Do I sound like the kind of cretin who packs envelopes?"

But I'm screaming into a dead line. The guy at the help desk is not paid to take scorching abuse. He's gone.

Breathe, I say to myself, but fresh oxygen only stokes

the flamethrower. *Service economy, my sweet pert ass.* Yet another example of how my world spins out of control. I am being nibbled to death by ducks.

Fuck Art. Before I can write fiction, there is a world in need of correction. My complaint letters absorb all my creative energy.

In this Digital Age, I have reduced being a pain in the ass to an efficient science that merges linguistic elegance with typography and graphics. I bolt boilerplate paragraphs into broadsides of scorn. With boldface, underlining, and italics, I savage newspapers, government agencies, and corporate offices. I may not control idiots, but I can be certain they will know they are idiots. Who has time for imagining fiction? My letters are withering prose poems, evocative, provocative, sarcastic, witty, turn on clever rhetorical questions, and conclude with inescapable logic that the reader is inept. Resignation, as a matter of honor, is required. My metaphors drip disdain. The letters all start with the same sentence in italicized capital letters: *I AM NOT A CRANK!* CEOs will read them aloud to shamed vice-presidents. I am nuts enough to wonder how I might publish a bestselling collection of those letters. Will Knopf be interested? I also imagine the reviews: *Amusing! Accurate!* and *Piercing social commentary that plumbs the temper of our times!*

This latest letter of focused fury to the inept mutual fund takes a mere ninety caffeinated minutes to compose. I read the penultimate draft to Debi, my wife of eight years. She folds laundry. Our bedroom smells of Clorox. When a phrase fails to drop trippingly off my tongue, I pause to pencil a correction, but as my eyes finally lift from the paper, I see Debi trembling.

Panic flits in her pale blue eyes. She's tethered to a maniac. She turns to me, lifts her eyes and barely whispers, "I have to tell you....I'm a lesbian."

Debi is short and physically frail, and I have grown large with compulsive eating. Might I become violent?

I have stumbled over her secret. She diverts her money to a psychiatrist. To leave no paper trail at work, she pays in cash.

Miraculously, in a rare moment of clarity, I rise above the reflexive asshole I've become in the decade since I left Iowa. As she confesses, I clearly see Debi, my good wife. "This must be so hard for you," I say. My arms encircle her.

Debi has endured volcanic rage for so long, my unexpected compassion blindsides her. She falls against me to weep with relief. Of course, I don't want her to move out. Of course, we'll go at this together. Of course. Of course. Nothing could be more important.

Debi's announcement disinters the better man I once was.

This best moment with my second wife is also the worst moment of our marriage, maybe the worst in all my life. I love her, but I will lose her.

Fact is she is already lost.

As a writer, I construct narratives to explain what seems inexplicable. As a literary artist, I commit those narratives in language in arrangements that feel true and beautiful. As a matter of discipline, in these memoirs, I limit myself to facts, though not to chronology.

Look how this story begins so close to its end. You'll have to stay alert for any of it to make meaning. Memory is not serial. By deliberate arrangement of the narrative and by careful selection of language, I seduce you into conspiring with me to make sense of what we both should know has no explanation. Literature is an illusion of order. Years and days begin and end on schedules made by clocks and calendars. Those, too, are illusions. Wars begin and end by decree, but there is no end to time nor closure for the dead. Life just goes forward. It can have no purpose.

So be forewarned: this final riff on love delivers no satisfactory conclusion. As I said in this book's first riff, I just report. Go back and reread it if you've forgotten. Pay some goddam attention. I was not kidding.

If you insist on believing the writer's job is to supply closure, you will say, "Glasser, you cannot present a story you do not understand. Think it through and get back to us."

Why do you think I sit here typing?

Fiction is neat; life sloppy. This account is what it is. I will not imagine light where there is shadow; I sound no bells in fog. Sloppy is my métier.

II

Were this fiction, it would be a love story. We'd begin on a certain cloudless late September day beneath the blue dome of Heaven back in greenest Iowa. Debi had a life before that. I had a life before that. Still, every narrative begins somewhere, and this moment offers itself, better than most.

For Dickens, beginnings are often a birth. Other writers begin tales with an arrival or a departure. Push off on a raft. Set sail in pursuit of the great whale. My amateur student writers are enamored of mechanical alarm clocks inevitably hurled against a wall—a new day! Only fairy tales take place in a perpetual present, *Once upon a time*. For Shakespeare, action begins with a disruption of order. Time goes out of joint because of supernatural intervention that triggers someone's defect in character, unnatural jealousy, overleaping ambition, or a tragic tendency to think too much. "Yo, Hamlet, the ghostie on the parapet at midnight says he's your old man, wants to chat." "Ignore those three weird sisters, Mac; nothing good will come of telling your wife what they predict." But by the end of five acts, corpses litter the stage and order is restored, pleasing royal patrons who feared betrayal and social disruption more than they feared plague.

Storytelling. Nothing to it. Nothing beats it. Neat as can be. Beginning, middle, end. Just like your life and mine, right? where each and every day is neatly partitioned from every other and your purposes clear to everyone and even yourself.

Well, maybe not.

So for this love story, "Perry and Debi," you deliver yourself to artifice. Accept that this love story has its beginning.

On that early fall day, the Iowa horizon seems near enough to touch, but no matter how long we drive on those ruler-straight roads, the world's edge draws no closer. We're in Debi's gun-gray Volkswagen Rabbit, a hand-me-down vehicle from her mother that could stand a better muffler. The humid air flowing through the open windows is pungent with hay, tall corn, and what I have already learned during my first three months in the world's bread box is what farmers call *the smell of money* and what I mistakenly call *the stink of shit*.

"I used to detassel corn," Debi says. Her eyes go from the road to me to discover if her new friend from New York City understands her. I confess I am clueless, so Debi informs me that corn stalks have male and female parts, that high school kids snip tassels to prevent the willy-nilly pollination of next year's valuable, genetically pure seed. It's hard work, impossible for a machine. Hot sun, broad-brimmed straw hats, "Chiggers everywhere. Yuck." She shivers.

What in hell is a chigger? "You castrate plants?"

Debi laughs, makes a scissors of her fingers, and says, "Snip, snip." Speaking of castration, though, she tells me yet another story about her grandfather's Montana ranch where she bottle-fed orphaned lambs. Out among the cattle, there'd come a day when lesser bulls had to become steers for much the same reason corn had to be detasseled. Cotton and corn and cows do not fall in love; they fertilize indiscriminately. Had I ever eaten Rocky Mountain Oysters? Debi swears she had a pet cow, Blackie. When Debi was six, she rode the lumbering animal's back.

She takes this stuff for granted; as a boy who came

of age in a poolroom, I am charmed and fascinated.

The Volkswagen carries us north to Ankeny, a town with few reasons to exist other than the snow-white grain elevators at its center, stark and in bold relief against that cobalt sky, the same color of Debi's astonishing eyes. The Des Moines Area Community College is at the town's outskirts. Debi calls the school "Deemack," and I am a citizen of Iowa for months before I realize people articulate the acronym—DMACC.

We pass Urbandale. We pass Clive. Debi wonders aloud why so many Midwestern towns are named for their water towers, and the joke, old to her and new to me, makes us laugh. For the first time I am exposed to the very Midwestern idea that a joke told once is best told again and again, familiarity making it all the more amusing in the retelling. A good joke is like fine wine or cheese: better with age and always shared.

Debi is 26. The semester before I arrived in Iowa, Drake University awarded Debi her Masters in English. The same semester, Drake awarded her mother, Dorothy, an advanced degree in Art Therapy. The photograph of the two smiling women in caps and gowns made the newspaper's front page. Mother and daughter have the same face. I later learn that I am closer to her mother's age than I am to Debi's.

We met at an English Department pre-semester gathering, my first genuine social interaction in Des Moines, a welcome change from strolling through a shopping mall just to be among people. I arrived in mid-August and while waiting for my furniture to catch up to me spent a week sleeping on a thin towel

I'd stolen from a motel in North Platte, Nebraska.

As a rule, English professors are married, middle-aged, potbellied, and prefer books to conversation, but at the department gathering people are eager to meet the intense New York Jew, curly-haired and blonde, trim, athletic, a young professor whose pre-arrival publicity is about his creativity and talent. Debi and I pass on the street a day later, and after a few minutes of cordial talk as we part I ask if she wants to sometime have lunch. She says "Yes," but before I am at the end of the block I spin to call back over my shoulder, "Dinner?" and when she hollers, "Yes," again, I push my luck once more and shout, "Tonight?"

Over milk and pie at a diner, she confesses her aberrant interest in Lois Lane and Wonder Woman. When her young professor date names no fewer than four colors of Kryptonite and identifies each one's effects on Superman, Debi discovers that Lex Luthor, Bizarro, and Glasser are old buddies. On long rainy days at summer camp I read comics with 10¢ cover prices. Debi is chagrined to learn that I stupidly bent the spines backward before tossing them into the trash. *Why didn't you keep them?* She prattles on about comic book conventions where acne-ridden adolescent boys grow tongue-tied in her presence, a woman.

We start seeing each other. We start seeing each other a lot. I feel obliged to tell her that so soon after a divorce, I will be seeing other women. While this does not thrill her, she accepts it.

So much for deep background. Let's get back to that

beginning.

That Saturday on which this love story begins, Debi propels the Volkswagen through the empty elliptical streets of DMACC until, brakes squealing, we stop before one of several glass houses. Debi rummages through her purse, then dumps the bag's contents. No luck. She searches on the floor of the car.

"I'm really sorry," she says, crestfallen. "I forgot the key."

We are bound for a picnic after she finishes this chore, but now it seems our plans for Saylorville Dam are blown. Debi would never consider skipping watering the plants. Debi being Debi, she is responsible. One of her mother's former husbands is the school's horticulturist. Debi calls him "Dad." In Debi's world, the plants are watered when they need to be watered. Not yesterday. Not tomorrow. Today. She cannot let Dad down. "We'll have to drive back and turn around and drive back again," she says.

So I ask if she has any tools. In her car trunk, under some rags, we discover an old screwdriver with a chipped blue plastic handle.

The greenhouse door is flimsy aluminum with at least a half-inch space between the frame and the door itself. I squat and see the bolt of the spring lock, shiny and worn with use. I brace the screwdriver against the bolt and open-palmed sharply rap the end of the handle. The jimmied aluminum door swings free on its hinges. When we leave, the door will lock behind us, undamaged.

"How did you do that?" Debi says.

"I'm from Brooklyn," I say as we go inside. "Boys did not detassel corn, but we learned breaking and entering."

The inside of the greenhouse is hot, damp, and smells of rot. I've never been in a greenhouse, so in that moment, being who I am, I rethink the opening of Raymond Chandler's *The Big Sleep*; Marlowe, a detective, meets General Sternwood, a dying, bloodless man who raises hothouse orchids and promiscuous daughters. Sternwood comments on "the sweet smell of corruption."

Debi swings a hose with a showerhead attached to the nozzle, soaking what looks to me like racks of rhododendrons. Rivulets of water trickle to the floor and flow through shallow concrete runoff channels. I expect her to spray me, but "cute and playful" is not her style. I like that. Coy women make me tired. Maybe she thinks I am an "older" man, 36, so she does not want to come across as a kid. Her near-blonde curly hair is shoulder length; her lips achingly thin and colorless; her nose comes to a point. Coming toward you in a railroad station, you'd probably not turn your head to see her go by.

That would be your loss.

The granddaughter of a Congregationalist minister who on Sundays preached on a circuit, traveling among four churches by buckboard, Debi was born when her mother, Dorothy, was fifteen. By the time Debi was eight, she performed housekeeping, cooking and child-rearing chores for two younger siblings.

Why mess with dolls when Mom supplied real human beings that needed attention? When her mother gathered up her three children and struck out on her own, Debi had no choice but to become her mother's best friend and confidante, not to mention the steadier hand for the family's emotional trials. There were plenty of those. Debi became her family's emotional pivot.

Debi's birth was no consequence of a youthful indiscretion. In Montana, womenfolk are harvested when prime. Debi is the first of three children sired by Dorothy's rancher husband, a disturbed and disturbing man I met only once. Debi's and her sister's eyes rolled in panic at any mention of the bitter court battle in which their mother won custody of her two daughters and son. They were young children then; nevertheless, as adults, a phone call from Ed would send two otherwise levelheaded women into tailspins.

Free of her husband, Debi's mother, Dorothy, fled from Red Lodge, Montana, to a trailer park in Cody, Wyoming. She found work with a florist. One day, the shop's front door's Christmas bells jingled in a professor of Horticulture. As best I can ascertain, soon after, the family moved to Iowa. I may have some details wrong: the hegira is sketchy. In Iowa, Dorothy shed her plant professor, but I cannot say how long they were married or how close on that divorce Dorothy married husband number three. He, too, was an older man, a man of purported wealth whose money turned out to be swamp gas.

Some time after we married, Debi's biological father passed through Massachusetts. Ed was educated as a geologist, but that did not explain why he poured so much sugar onto his Frosted Flakes that a small mountain of granules peaked higher than the rim of the bowl. For three meals each day, he ate nothing else except hardboiled eggs.

He dined at our breakfast table after a short detour from his Greyhound bus journey from Montana to Washington D.C. He was no tourist. Once in the nation's capitol, he planned to reveal to the government of the United States of America the injustice running rampant in Big Sky country. He'd lost the family ranch in an inheritance battle, and so in person he would deliver directly to the F.B.I. the news of collusion to defraud among a vast network of judges, lawyers, press, legislators, and title offices. He had evidence that his unanswered letters were being intercepted, opened, joshed at, and burned. Every official in Montana, including postal employees, was for sale and had been bought.

Ed seemed not to hear his daughter's three-times-posed question as to whether he had an appointment with any federal officer.

After a night at our place, we drove him to the Boston bus terminal. The last I ever saw of the thin man with a sweat-stained gray Bailey hat, he stood curbside, a nylon gym-bag of clothing slung from one shoulder, a white paper sack that held the four hard-boiled eggs he'd prepared on our stove clutched in his rough hand.

I remember thinking, *What kind of lunatic sends letters like that?*

Placed as it is, it's tempting to seize upon such a narrative as presenting some basis for what would become Debi's shift in sexuality, all that geographic displacement, a mother moving from husband to husband, an unstable father. The artist finds the irony of my thinking that a man intent on pleading his case with the FBI by letters and then in person must be addled. The reader draws lines of connection, those lines that make meaning beyond mere anecdote.

Told in chronological time, no such artistic effects are possible. Proximity on the page, the chronology of memory, makes meaning possible. In real time, it will take years before the nutcase writing letters will be me, so had I begun this riff in the greenhouse among the rhododendrons and moved forward from there, poor Ed's lunacy, far from the beginning and far from the ending, would only seem a comic interlude at best. Debi's classic dysfunctional family must have troubled her—too young, she served as her mother's adult companion, a role reversal that can and does precipitate any amount of grief. But it will take decades before she will discover or acknowledge she is a lesbian, so when I select the detail of her family background to present to you, I do so that you might perceive cause and effect.

That, too, is an illusion. Perception of cause and effect in matters of the heart can never be trusted.

The truth of the origins of Debi's shifting sexual preference will remain the clouded mystery of this tale. Her sexual preference seems to have shifted, but maybe Debi was who she was from birth and the woman watering the hothouse rhododendrons was in denial, experimenting with heterosexuality, and I was the experiment.

A more manipulative writer could invent a scene that shows mother and daughter closely allied, suggesting the daughter will reiterate the mother's marital patterns, fleeing to ever more successful men. That Volkswagen suggests itself as a symbol: once her mother's mechanism for movement, it became Debi's. Perhaps for symbolism's sake, the more manipulative writer might make more of that newspaper photograph of the two women with one face. They are posed in dual profile, facing each other like mirror reflections.

You see how meaning and sense are matters of design? I organize events and facts on the page, choosing what to put in and what to leave out, so you can withdraw meaning from it. Every competent writer does the same.

But like good writing, memory is also selective. More complicated, memory is never linear. Print marches along like so many ants on a path the writer selects and the reader follows. Artfully managed, we arrive together at a contrived conclusion, the art being to occlude any sense of contrivance.

Here, I've told you what I know. If it helps, I'll add that Debi's mother, Dorothy, achieved independence by hanging out a shingle as an art therapist. She specialized in advising abused women to grab their kids, get out, run like hell, and never look back.

If you think it will help you to impose meaning, know too that good, gentle Debi significantly differs from her mother in her ability to accept risk. She's no adventuress, but where Dorothy's life was reactive, Debi's is proactive.

Were I a fiction writer, I'd cultivate the irony that makes so fine aesthetic resonance: a lesbian came to acknowledge her nature after a decade by traipsing 1,500 miles to marry a man. You'd insist that I invent a scene or two to underscore the pathos of that journey and the parallels between a geographic journey and the wandering of the heart. I'd be obliged to render Debi's gradual realization of who she is and who she must become. If I were bold enough, the art of that unwritten tale would be delicate and complicated; the emotional pitch a subtle soupçon of vague guilt and half-articulated sexual attractions never fully realized. Any decent hack should be able to muster up the needed sensibility.

But I have no knowledge of such moments, and I will not turn this love story into fodder for a trendy novel marketed with that most odious of taglines, "based on true events." Really, what fiction was ever written that was not?

Enough already. I've already supplied you an initial scene at a greenhouse that at once shows the lovers' affinity in a locale that is fertile but redolent of rot. I roped in an inappropriate reference to a novel by Raymond Chandler just to underscore the point. We've filled in some exposition via narrative flashback that traces the history of Debi's forebears. That's plenty.

The exposition being done, the love story wants development, complex characterization to make subsequent action explicable.

A few deft scenes ought to do. This is where a reviewer too dull to think of anything else to say will admire the writer's "fine eye for telling detail." We can't spend too long here—we also need to advance the damned plot, get to a climax and then suggest some conclusion that, incredibly, should connect to the Jefferson Airplane.

Let us get on with it.

III

During my second arctic Iowa winter, at Winter Break when Jessica flies off to her mother in Tucson, Debi and I flee to Las Vegas. We enjoy the desert heat; we enjoy the shows. I linger at blackjack, but Debi's adventurous spirit draws a line at gambling. She drops a few quarters into slot machines, grunts appreciatively to learn that before they became electronic they were called one-armed-bandits, but that's all the gambler Debi will ever be.

Debi undertakes her most serious risk in the coffee shop of the Stardust. I order a Crenshaw melon. She knows cantaloupe; she knows honeydew. "What's that?" she asks, and before I can answer, she stabs her fork at the pre-sectioned crescent of golden melon on my plate, spears a piece, devours it, slides my plate in front of her, and steals my midnight breakfast. A year or two later, soon after I move to New England, before she comes to stay, she visits and tastes her first lobster. She downs five lobsters in three days.

In her life, food adventures are not small escapades: her mother, sister and brother live on a diet of anything white—Wonder Bread, vanilla ice cream, Vienna Fingers, baked potato, rice, Miracle Whip. Her brother will essay fried shrimp, though scallops, despite being the requisite color, may as well be garden slugs.

These selected details illustrate personality, but they also have a not terribly subtle subtext: Debi sees in me a connection to a broader, wider, more cosmopolitan world than any she might ever know in Iowa. We had profound differences, but those differences gave us the strength of an alloy.

Make no mistake. Debi was not premeditatedly climbing from a well of Midwestern provincialism and I was no rope ladder. Debi simply needed more than Iowa could offer, but she was no opportunist or plotter.

One road to meaning is to ponder the story not written. Any competent writer could invent any number of plot lines for Debi without recourse to someone like me appearing in her life. In Chapter Two, Debi makes the dramatic break from her encompassing family for which she has always been too responsible; she loads all of her possessions into that rusted Volkswagen and drives to Big City, Anywhere. The heroines of *Moll Flanders* and *Pamela* did no less. Modern variations are either hilarious or tragic. *Rubyfruit Jungle* meets *Sister Carrie*. Set the novel in New York, give Debi an improbable job at a magazine or book publisher, any setting where eccentric but smart people come and go and Debi can sit at a desk in air-conditioned comfort. On the jacket copy, make certain at least one blurb contains the word *hysterical*. The novel will deliver at least one joke about menstruation, a lot of angst about shoes that require a second mortgage for purchase, and women in anguish about cultivating good relationships, though none of Debi's friends will want to fall in love. *Relationships* imply control; *love* implies the loss of will.

But this is no novel. Let's persist with what dear old sexless Henry James called the "futility of facts."

I've brought from Tucson my running habit learned from Brenda, the Girl Scout calendar cover girl with the 38-inch inseam, my Valkyrie of the Desert. Debi tells me she, too, exercises regularly. She is short, wears a petite 2, is narrow in the chest, but her arms and legs are lean without being stocky.

Debi and I run the perimeter of the university campus. It's nice to run with someone whose stride matches my own. The oppressive Iowa summer sun sucks water from the black earth so hard and so fast that all that is at issue is whether the five o'clock thunderstorm will birth a tornado or merely pelt the earth with hail large enough to dimple autos. Weightlifting and running, I am in the best physical condition of my life. I run shirtless, tanned, my cotton gym shorts slit at the seams to leave unrestrained my bulked-up thighs.

While we jog, Debi and I talk, a sure sign of fitness, but on the second circuit Debi first becomes silent and then slightly staggers. We stop in the shade of an oak. I run in place. Debi wears Tretorns, black nylon shorts, and a pink running shirt. We shine with healthy sweat. She reaches for the tree, but her limp hand never finds it. As she mutters, "I just need a minute," she faints, but I catch her.

I lift her in my two arms like the hero I long to be. Debi's arms droop about my neck. Her head flops against my chest. Her eyelids flutter. I carry her three city blocks to my rented house where I gently place her on the backyard grass in the house's shadow, the same spot where I will soon build a tetherball court for Jessica. Debi leans back on her elbows, babbling something brave about how this has never happened to her before. I bring her ice, water, and a damp washcloth. I cradle her neck while she takes slow sips.

After a while, I carry her inside, put her in my bed, pull a crisp white sheet to her chin, and she curls into a ball to sleep five hours. At the time, I hardly think of it as anything extraordinary. Who wouldn't carry a woman a quarter mile in high heat and care for her? When she wakes, she says, "What happened?" I tell her. Her eyes widen round and blue as café crockery.

My first time in her tiny apartment, she offers me a drink. She scrambles onto the kitchen counter and like an acrobatic crab scurries sideways to reach the uppermost cabinet above the refrigerator where a half-bottle of Johnny Walker hides among seldom-used pots and pans. Dust covers the red label. She leaps to the floor, rinses a water glass, and pours scotch as if she poured milk. The rituals of ice or moderation are unknown to her. The one time we dine at a relatively fancy restaurant, with true linen tablecloths and no flickering electric lights but honest wax candles burning in glass globes, Debi hazards a half-glass of wine. As I drive us home, Debi near tumbles out of the passenger side of my yellow Chevette, she is so loopy.

She gets the giggles. I do, too. When Debi laughs, she laughs for so long her eyes tear, and that makes her laugh more. It's a special phenomenon I come to seek. When Debi laughs, no one within earshot can resist laughing with her.

After a childhood overburdened with responsibility and her education as a classical musician, Debi develops a taste for the lowbrow music she hears around me. Debi buys Motown albums. She discovers Aretha Franklin. She learns that what Drake University's Marching Band calls Band Riff #2 is the opening of "Can't Turn You Loose," the Otis Redding number where he is backed by Booker T. and the MGs. She is surprised to learn the Grateful Dead neither scream nor wear lurid costumes, but do odd things with tempo, mandolins, drums, and syncopation. When Debi hears me sing, she swears I have perfect pitch. The only musical instrument I can play is my stereo, but despite my being sure she says such things to flatter me, my ego swells and I sing to her when we drive, bellowing terrible songs.

Toto doing "Africa?" Really?

Guided by my Midwestern Beatrice, I come to appreciate the slower pace of people for whom any civil interchange requires two ceremonial refusals before acceptance.

Will you have coffee?
I'm just fine.
Just a small cup?
No, thank you.
I'm making coffee for myself.
Well, all right then, if it's no trouble, a small cup will do for me.

Seeing the world through Debi's blue eyes, I come to shed my New York City provincialism, that arrogance that presumes the inferiority of every other place. My mind broadens. Perhaps the city-boy is less worldly that the buckboard minister's granddaughter.

I am in love in the Heartland.

IV

Exposition and characterization accomplished, a good love story embarks on complications. The essence of drama is conflict. Lovers must struggle. With no obstacles, there is no drama, and with no drama, a story is no story.

Constancy is not my priority. I'd never been an unmarried adult. I told Debi early on, "I owe it to myself to go out with more than one person." I know me. If I am someday to have a stable life, I need this.

It's that code again: Protect the weak; do not lie for advantage.

Good soul, Sweet Debi endures my tomcatting. For the three years I am in Iowa, Debi and I travel together; when Jessica first visits from Arizona, Debi teaches my child to ice skate. The following year, when Jessica permanently joins me, the three of us take up bicycling.

Debi does everything right; nevertheless, rumors wander back to her—many true. You've read a few of those tales in this book, and the tales presented here are by no means comprehensive.

Code, schmode: Debi suffers predictable anguish. Is she inadequate? What can she do she isn't doing?

To make the drama perfectly transparent, a screenwriter would create an obligatory moment on page 30 of a 120-page script. On that page, Debi must articulate precisely what Debi wants, supplying the audience with unequivocal understanding of what is at stake. Scarlet O'Hara swears, "I will never be hungry again!" Rocky Balboa confesses, "I just wanna go the distance." The entire cast sings, "Fame! I want to live forever!"

Look, if you need uncluttered vision, rent a DVD. Life, however, is sloppy.

Debi suffers, but she does so mostly in silence. Maybe she has romantic alternatives in Des Moines about which I know nothing, arms that hold her and supply solace and affection. Maybe those arms are female. Perhaps she suffers far less than I imagine.

Fiction writers presume omniscience. I just report, and I will not invent "facts."

As my time in Iowa draws to a close, as a parent, lover, and writer, I come to rely on Debi's strength. I value her more than she suspects.

A few weeks before I depart for my new job at yet another college Debi's mother and sister invite Debi and me to dinner. Jessica is in Arizona, set to fly back to Daddy once I am settled in Massachusetts. Have no doubt, Debi's sister and Dorothy have been through three years of my crap with Debi. They know most, if not the worst, and they are there not only to say goodbye to her boyfriend, the Jewish writer, teacher, father, athlete and committed bachelor, but also to begin to afford Debi the emotional support she will need to send me packing in order to heal her heart.

We order dessert. Dorothy conversationally asks, "What will you miss about Iowa?"

What will I miss? The climate? My first winter in Des Moines sets records for cold; the second winter breaks all the records set the previous winter, so frigid that one of my nylon auto tires freezes out of round. I've steered Debi's car from Omaha to Des Moines through whiteout conditions. No, I will not miss the climate.

What will I miss? Opportunities? My three years in Iowa, the farm economy has been wrecked. Farmers auction land to live, sell equipment to pay debt, and Willie Nelson sings for Farm-Aid. I have intoned headlines to Debi, "Jew in Iowa—Property Values Plummet"; Debi laughs hard enough that her eyes tear. Giddily I put forward the proposition that the people who settled the Northern Plains must be the descendants of incompetent pioneers. Making their way to California or Oregon, places worth going to, the wagons collapsed. "They had to eat the ox," I say. No, I will not miss opportunities.

What will I miss? These three women have every

expectation that I will answer Dorothy's question with a snappy comment they can and will repeat in conversations that begin, *Remember good old Perry?*

But during my time in Iowa, I've loved, I've parented, I've worked, I've created. I don't know what more I could want, except for one thing.

So when Dorothy with a light in her eyes says, "What will you miss about Iowa?" I instantly respond, "Debi. I'll miss Debi. The only thing I'll miss in Iowa is Debi."

They wait for the never delivered punch line. Debi's eyes brim.

V

In every love story, the lovers part and reunite. How else to know the full value of what they have?

Distance makes our love intensify. Every Sunday, I hover over *The Boston Globe* want-ads circling jobs for her. She visits Jessica and me several times. Our phone bills and her airline fare come to more than her rent. Miraculously, a hospital in New Hampshire flies her in to interview for a corporate communication job, and when they hire her, Debi is out of excuses.

Her brother helps her make the 1,700 mile drive in that Volkswagen; they arrive with a flat tire. I roast a chicken. Her brother is astonished I can cook. He says, "Pretty good," after he devours most of the seven-pound bird. A day later, his ticket purchased by Debi, he wings for home.

I am done chasing women. I have found all the love I will ever need.

For a while, this love story continues just as you might hope. Five years after we met, two after Debi comes to Massachusetts, we return to Iowa to exchange vows in a civil ceremony held in her mother's living room.

I am filled with hope and certainty.

I don't need to invent scenes from the marriage to underscore the point. Truth works for me.

Debi rings the doorbell and stands in the doorframe like a homeless waif. She is weeping. She's been fired. We are not yet married, and she is terrified of being a financial burden. My Midwestern, ever-earnest girlfriend whom I taught to balance a checkbook has never heard of unemployment insurance. Ever-worldly Perry reassures her. It's not welfare. She will not have to stand in long lines to answer humiliating questions, nor will she be forced to accept a job that requires a hairnet. The check arrives by mail. All she need do is cash it.

For the next six months, when she is not telephoning business buddies or packing envelopes with her resume, she spends hours at our health club surrounded by blonde wood, mirrors, and ferns while she climbs a treadmill set at an angle steeper than Mt. McKinley. You'd think she was training for the triathlon. Debi comes to believe the Bataan Death March should be a tourist attraction. She muses about ditching her education and becoming an aerobics instructor. But Debi does not have it in her to be an idler. A job comes her way and she feels obligated to take it, but when I persuade her to pass, she is doubtful. "The salary doesn't value you enough," I say. Weeks later and another 10,000 miles on the treadmill, another far more lucrative and fulfilling offer comes her way.

This is what committed lovers do. Confidence. Support. Debi's career soars. She accepts risk and jumps from job to job eventually becoming an executive. She is not yet 40.

In the happy story this is not, love and marriage would grow ever more profound until we finish each other's sentences.

That's no novel. Where is the drama? It's more like the home video shown at our 50th wedding anniversary party, after which our kids present us with the tickets to embark on a world cruise where we will watch from the fantail a sun ripe as a peach slowly sinks into the blue Aegean.

Life, unlike cruise ships, turns on a dime.

I don't refer to Debi's change in sexual orientation. I am bewildered whether that is cause or effect. No, our ruin germinates long before I am aware of Debi's changes, if that is indeed what they were.

Take a breath. This love story's subplot will submerge us into the darkest corridors of madness and obsession.

VI
When the garden flowers baby are dead yes
and your mind is full of red
Don't you want somebody to love?

Bradford College. A smarter man would have headed for an exit. I could have run a fruit stand, enrolled in bartending school, or, like my father, spackled walls. You know, instead of being an academic with literary pretensions, I could have made an honest living.

I stayed ten years.

College teaching has undeniable seductions—June, July and August, to name just three; the admiration of youth and mild levels of prestige to name two more. But I am in a dead end job at a college that confuses professors with galley slaves. We are lashed to the oars and pull to an ever quickening cadence under the threat of bankruptcy. The fact that Bradford College would supply none of the perquisites of college teaching was soon evident.

At my job interview, I was asked to join a crusade; this tiny community would be the academy on the hill, a laboratory for the crisis facing Higher Education, the relevance of the liberal arts. My position as the house writer will be the centerpiece of this strategy. What this means in practice is perpetual curriculum revision and endless meetings, including summers. Later I learn that all my colleagues have been seduced by the academy on the hill speech and all have been told they will be college's future centerpiece.

After three years, knowing Bradford is on the verge of disaster, I make it my personal mission to save the place.

I am crazy enough to think this possible; I am trapped enough by history to see no alternative.

A digression. This subplot's narrative is already careening out of control, so why not?

The riff began with a scene near the end of my second marriage, flashed us back to a moment in a greenhouse, filled in the origins of a love story, anecdotally supplied characterization, alluded to Debi's childhood and origins, offered some poignant moments leading to a wedding, but now instead of hammering home to closure will veer into the self-serving Saga of the Angry White Guy.

Subplots present structural challenges. A love story has an arbitrary beginning that Art can persuade you is the rightful start, but though the subplot need not begin at the same moment, it must conclude simultaneous to the mainline. How much to explain? How far back shall I go? Writing and reading are linear, but memory is a shapeless gestalt.

More challenging: subplot suggests simultaneity—an impossibility for narrative text, unless you can read one story with your left eye and another with your right.

Most challenging: the Angry White Guy does not trust all his own faculties. We are in the black swamp of literature: the unreliable narrator.

Here is the deal: I won't lie to you. I will not exaggerate.

If you do not buy the interpretations, remember, I was there.

Start with some additional characterization.

You must by now have noticed how often I forward discount my heart's needs. Today's wheat is tomorrow's bread, but I hoard grain and rarely bake, starving now to hedge against an imagined risk-free future.

No such thing, but who knew?

Teach now, avoid the draft, write later—a decade passes like smoke dispelled by high wind.

Marry now, build a life, fall in love later—another decade pissed away while my soul is corrupted and damage done to Helena.

Take custody of Jessica now, raise her securely by teaching, commit to Art later—I'd do it again in a minute, but there is no denying the cost of the delay.

And here came Bradford College in Massachusetts, just as I rounded 40. The place where I was supposed to settle. It was a flyspeck of a school with 425 students, a summer camp that awarded academic credits for hefty fees, worth every dime if your troubled kid needed a regularly delivered motivating kick in the ass.

The students were great, but as an academic community Bradford was dysfunctional.

I am required to attend semester-opening consciousness-raising workshops where hired guns called *sensitivity trainers* closely and publicly question me, a white male, about my innate racism. I refuse to confess. They become exasperated.

No, I do not respond to minority students differently. I call my attitude "professionalism." That does not stop the auto-da-fé. Why don't I admit I harbor racist thoughts? Everyone else has.

My colleagues were educated in privileged enclaves such as Smith, Trinity, Swarthmore, and Vassar at about the same time I had been cajoling black and Puerto Rican girls to read and write and maybe take an AP class, but no one at Bradford knows that or wants to ponder what that means. It would upset their worldview: racism is assumed. If they knew I'd taught James Joyce and Bernard Shaw to Hispanic and black 17-year-olds, they'd assume it was part of some imperial-colonial plot. If they knew I'd slept with a Puerto Rican who attended but did not graduate from Harvard, they'd assume exploitive rape.

My colleagues believe the poor are the vanguard of a force that will make the needed changes to the system, a lesson they learned at Smith, Trinity, Swarthmore, and Vassar, those enclaves safely sheltered from the poor and disenfranchised. Of course, they cannot know what I learned from a woman who scrubbed bathroom floors at night who leaned close to whisper that she relied on me to teach her daughter everything I knew and more so that her daughter could have my job. She did not want to change the system so much as get her piece of it.

My interrogation goes on through an entire morning. I am isolated at lunch. I skip the afternoon session. The next week my dean notes my half-day absence and sternly explains my presence had been required.

At one faculty meeting when I ask exactly who is in charge of naming which groups have been marginalized and so now need compensating privilege,

I am informed that unlike other groups that will receive preferred admissions, scholarships, and hiring bonuses, Jews are oppressors, part of the power structure. I think of my daughters' relatives up the flumes of Dachau and Treblinka. "Who'd have guessed Hitler had it right all along?" I ask. Exasperated colleagues roll their eyes. What a pain in the ass this obstructionist Glasser is. How does anyone with his head so far up his ass publish so much?

At yet another meeting about faculty personnel, the postulate is presented that too few gays are on the faculty. Never mind it is illegal to ask, a few strident colleagues urge us unofficially to recruit along lines of sexual orientation. "When," I ask, "did we survey current faculty? How many homosexual encounters qualify a person as gay? How recently?" I start to give details about an experience I had at summer camp when I was 11 to ask whether it qualifies me to be included in the tally that ascertained our teaching needs, but I am shouted down.

A smarter Angry White Guy would have dropped his pants, bent forward, and fled for an exit, but I strap myself into the driver's seat for Bradford College's flaming death spiral, kidding myself into thinking that if I can reverse the stupidity of the college's culture, then I can create the ideal environment for myself. I allow myself to be elected to the head of faculty governance. I may be an obstructionist, sarcastic pain in the ass, a racist and reactionary prick, but when employment and salary issues are on the negotiating table, who better than the bellicose New York Yid to confront the administration?

Later, my shrink will tell me this was my first mistake, a common delusion that one can reconstruct one's environment, rather than reconstruct one's self. I do not have the courage it takes to be healthy.

Pride doesn't allow me to accept Debi's offer of support while I write. I persist in thinking I will shape my own life, much like I shape the lives of my fictional characters. Their lives are neat; my will be too.

So while I roll the rock of faculty governance, I stop writing. That temporary accommodation turns into years, and so once again I forward discount my heart's longing. Rather than confront my Art, I expect to save the college, save my job, and maybe save what is left of my mind.

That plan fails. As if it could ever succeed.

VII

As Grace Slick sang, *Your mind fills with red*.

Events have no sequence in my memory. The decade blurs in a haze of fury. Nothing affords me happiness or pleasure. Listen to the Jefferson Airplane song: the beat is nothing less than the pulse of a human heart. That's all I knew. My frustrations are so high, I hear the sound of a heart all the time, but it is not love. No, that's my elevated pulse in my ears. Anger makes my heart a tom-tom.

Jessica has the good fortune to attend prep school; she lives in a dorm, carries a backpack, and wears topsiders. She misses the worst, but when she is choosing a college I am far away, and while in a telephone booth at a writer's residence I deliver a tirade so loud and so vehement that when I exit the booth, people look away. Jessica ignores me and does as she wishes. She has grown used to my losses of control. Taking risk and being independent is what I raised her to do. She is on her own two-wheeler now.

Sweet Debi does not have the good fortune to be off at school.

Living with me is like being strapped to a gurney at the open door of a blast furnace. I don't have the excuse of being a drunk. All I have is omnipresent all-consuming anger.

I've lost control of my job and abandoned my Art; I've lost control of my body to diabetes and my daughter to maturity. I control nothing, least of all myself.

One day Debi returns from the market with a liter of Diet Coke. They've changed the design of the liter bottle. I ask, "What the fuck is this?" and she explains. "Take it back," I say. Her shoulders sag. In minutes, I am screaming. "Take the fucking thing back! It's goddam defective!" The veins in my throat swell. For hours, the firestorm of rage feeds on itself, sucking the oxygen from the room. My wife wilts before my eyes, but despite the plain harm I do her, I go on and on and on and on and on and on, helpless. A small soft voice at the back of my skull says *stop stop stop* but I cannot. As I write this more than a decade later, I wonder if poor Mad Beth, my suicide a decade earlier, had heard that same small voice when she mixed vodka with her lithium and showed me the blood oozing from the chessboard she had etched with a serrated steak knife on the smooth flesh of her underarm.

Diet fucking Coke?

The last threads of my life unravel. My brother and sister buy me a huge television as a birthday gift, and I hate it so much I scream about it for days. Everything is a 5-alarm fire; every day a Code 3, lights and sirens and pedal to the floor. While I abuse furniture and punch dents in our cheap walls, Debi learns to escape to another room. I deceive myself into believing my behavior is ordinary: I am Ralph Kramden, fist beneath Alice's chin and threatening to send her *Pow!* to the moon, the TV sit-com that neatly ended each episode with an embrace and a kiss. *Baby, you're the greatest.*

But Debi is no Alice; we are not *The Honeymooners*; sloppy life around me has no neat happy ending.

I never raise a hand to her, though Debi with her mother's history must calculate when I will. She fears what she sees coming.

It shames me to write that paragraph. My sole claim to virtue is that I never struck my wife.

My oldest friend, language, does not save me. Never mind my elegant boilerplate complaint letters, I mutter alone in my car, a perpetual court of appeals in session where my piercing prosecutions ridicule the fumbling defense, my scripts for testimonial showdowns and cross-examinations that can never come. *The bastards need to be told.* I am brilliant; my opponents beaten curs. I shame the idiots, the editors, students, colleagues, administrators, writers who publish when I do not, the motherfucking pricks who open my 300 job applications in seven years and gleefully shred them, my graduate school classmates whose careers flourish at lovely, nurturing schools where writers are honored. At my invitation, those sons-of-bitches were guests of Drake University or Bradford College before they had decent professorships, but once they settled in at better positions where they might return the favor, despite my having published two collections of fiction, they seem to misplace my telephone number.

In my sleep, I wrestle everything and everyone that besets me, and when I awaken, I am exhausted. Sleep brings no rest; dawn brings no hope.

I eat compulsively. Food is my narcotic. Once an athlete, I come to resemble the Hindenburg hovering over the flats of New Jersey, awaiting the lightning that will ignite me to burn. My body quits; I become diabetic. The headaches and dizziness without physical cause lead me to a shrink who prescribes Prozac. Since I cannot change jobs, he advises me to change careers. For the first time, I understand why alcohol is the disease of American letters.

Prozac leaves me emotionally numb and sexually uninterested, so I flush my supply down a toilet, but I give up even wanting to write, as well. Why write? What's the point? I am not dedicated to Art: I am a narcissistic careerist whose career is archaic.

Those 300 applications in seven years garner two interviews and no offers, the strident '80s a time when English departments will hire a woman who owns a pen before hiring a man who publishes books. I am white, urban, east coast, Jewish, male, unapologetically heterosexual; my type is a glut on the market, a generation late coming after Heller, Malamud, Roth, and Bellow. Never mind talent and ability, campus life is about vaginas, homosexuals, and people of color—the very criteria bandied about the faculty meetings at Bradford College. I am being trampled by history, the very same force I suggested to Helena made the difference between *goyim* and Jews. It's really just too bad for me. Wouldn't it be better for all concerned if I would just get out of the way?

When I try to write commercially, Fate makes a joke: I sell a young adult novel on the basis of a chapter and an outline. After six months of short nights and no weekends, I deliver the manuscript, collect the advance, and more than a year later a new editor asks for revisions. I deliver those in four more months. Another half year goes by, and another editor writes, this time to ask if I will please return the advance. She loves the book, but it is no longer what the house emphasizes, the house having been merged out of existence. I write a short note that politely reads, "Kiss my ass"; the book never sees print, and another nail is driven into my Bradford coffin.

Things suck. People suck. I suck.

The day I resign and begin my life as a magazine editor, I predict to Debi, "Bradford will be bankrupt in two years."

It takes three. After 197 years, the college rolls belly-up, victim of death by ideologues.

But it is too late for Debi; the damage is done. My health and my career are smoking wreckage. Sweet Debi is an unticketed passenger on the train wreck.

Thus, this whiny subplot finally reverts to the mainline.

VIII

You yawn and with some justice ask, "Glasser, what does this alleged subplot have to do with anything? Your life is hard; whose isn't? You become a prick, and so your wife longs to sleep with girls? Is that your claim? Do you expect laughter or contempt?"

You're right. You're right.

I'll stick with what I know, which is not enough. It's all I can do; it's all I have.

We are back to where this riff began.

Debi was 40-ish when she resumed her affair with a woman she'd known at 17. Or 16. Or 15. Something like that. Debi omitted mentioning her lesbian past to me—or is she bisexual?—maybe because she had suppressed it from her memory. It's comforting for me to believe that she never deliberately deceived me. Perhaps she could not reveal what she did not know.

But it is not impossible that for the whole of our marriage she led a double life. There were ghost phone calls when she first moved to join me and Jessica. I thought nothing of them, sure that any leftover relationships Debi had were at least half a continent behind her and so would die of neglect, but maybe the lovers never lost contact. Before deciding she hated teaching,

Debi did a semester at a community college; perhaps her lover was a former student and not an adolescent experiment.

But that is speculation. All I am willing to do is report. A coherent narrative requires a few invented scenes that I do not have handy. As I said, life is sloppy.

When facts are too painful or unknown, I retreat into my little chats about craft. Maybe you do not get Artistic Truth, but at least I am not wholly wasting your time.

I hope.

I can tell you that shortly after Debi and I separated, I found stacks of plastic telephone cards with a face value of near $1,000. She must have thought the deftly designed bits of plastic were collectibles, like her poly-bagged copies of *Wonder Woman* and *Lois Lane*. The cards allowed her to keep her calls to the Pacific Northwest and her friend off our phone bills, of course, but the cards also made me wonder. Debi's family had wandered like Lost Tribes over the northern central plains of a continent; it would take some doing to find a high school classmate after twenty years. Who found whom? Or was the relationship of more recent vintage?

There is a novel for you. Can an adolescent encounter stay emotionally vital for decades without renewal? Was it true love? Did my persistent fury push my wife to find an old flame? Or is that an irrelevant conceit manufactured by me for this riff when the fact is that true love for Debi simply appeared at an opportune time? I'd been an adulterer, but I did not marry with an adulterous partner at the ready. Might Debi have gone to the altar with a girlfriend aside and ready? Think of the furtive encounters, the hurried talks, the whispered devotions…those scenes are the elements of a page-turner. The moments write themselves. You don't need me to imagine them for you.

Debi agreed to stay under our roof until my mother was in the ground. How might I have explained to Muriel that her sonny-boy was losing Debi, whom she adored, because Debi preferred girls? Let her go to her grave convinced it was Joan Baez that had fucked up my life. So I pleaded that Debi do a little forward discounting. A Midwesterner, Debi always looked to the rearview mirror to admire the landscape she was leaving, so forward discounting the future was not her style. She delayed becoming the person she needed to be for my sake, a gracious act of charity for which I am still grateful.

Coda
Grace Slick tells me that when the truth is found to be lies, and all the joy within you dies, well, you want somebody to love.
At the opera's end, the tenor stands alone.

I could make up a happier ending to please you, but that would be pandering. My life—like yours, like anybody's, like everybody's—has no conclusion. Someday, it will simply stop, but that is no conclusion.
Imagining closure, resolution, and meaning are the

purposes of Art, not experience. *Art* comes from the same root as the words *artifice* and *artificial*. If you see purposes here, I am glad for you. Experience has no purpose.

Take that prior paragraph. The one you just read. Read it again should you need to. It's four short sentences.

The attentive reader will hear the echoes of the first metamemoir in this book, "Norwegian Wood." Those echoes might persuade that reader that reader and writer have come 'round full circle, completing a journey together.

That illusion of closure is nothing more than a shoddy trick any competent writer should be able to conjure.

Come, could the tale of a boy in a Brooklyn poolroom discovering the efficacy of ambiguity in Art in any way have presaged a divorce from a lesbian 35 years later? A nice guy, smart, funny, talented, an inspiring teacher, a *mensche* who plans for the future and who will step up to be a single father while delaying the fulfillment of his heart's desire—could there be meaning in any of this?

The day after we divorce, Debi and I simply return to our lives as they were. We each eat three meals. We market, stop at the dry cleaner, Jessica calls me to ask how I am feeling, I refuel my car, and I get ready for a week's work as a managing editor. When Debi and I divorced, a chapter did not end, no book was completed, no engaging episode was taped for broadcast at a later date.

Nothing starts or ends. Consciousness insists on labeling some moments *beginnings* and others *conclusions*. We cross the room while beneath our feet the planet spins. The planet travels an ellipse about the sun. The sun wheels at the galaxy's edge. The galaxy turns. Millions of galaxies fly through infinitely expanding space.

Einstein went to his grave unable to calculate a place at perfect rest, unable to prove that such a spot existed. There is no vantage point that affords superior perspective. The clockworks turns. There is no rest. Meaning is an illusion of order imposed by the mind, imprisoned in memory. The heart, however, chooses the more certain illusions we call love.

fin

CPSIA information can be obtained at www.ICGtesting.com
Printed in the USA
BVOW071623011112

304409BV00001B/1/P